Introducing the 36" Pro Line™ Cooktop with the cooking power of 15,000 BTUs. Combine it with five-ply Stainless Steel Cookware and the legendary Stand Mixer, and you'll never want to sleep in again. For our Lemon Soufflé Pancakes recipe, and to view the entire KitchenAid® line, visit www.KitchenAid.com, or call 1.800.422.1230.

FOR THE WAY IT'S MADE.™

day*by*day

Front cover: Cinnamon Rolls, page 11; photography by Howard L. Puckett; styling by Ashley J. Wyatt; and food styling by Jan A. Smith

Editor: **Alyson Moreland Haynes**
Art Director: **Clare T. Minges**
Assistant Foods Editor: **Regan Jones, R.D.**
Copy Editor: **Jacqueline Giovanelli**
Editorial Assistant: **Allison Long**
Contributing Editor: **Kate McWhorter**
Editorial Interns: **Jennifer Kalinowski, R.D., Jane Lorberau**
Publishing Systems Administrator: **Rick Tucker**

Photographers: **Ralph Anderson, Jim Bathie, Tina Cornett, Colleen Duffley, Brit Huckabay, Becky Luigart-Stayner, Randy Mayor, Howard L. Puckett**
Photo Stylists: **Cindy Manning Barr, Kay E. Clarke, Melanie J. Clarke, Virginia R. Cravens, Mary Catherine Muir, Fonda Shaia, Ashley J. Wyatt**

Test Kitchens Director: **Elizabeth Luckett**
Assistant Director: **Julie Christopher**   Recipe Editor: **Gayle Hays Sadler**
Test Kitchens Staff: **Gretchen P. Feldtman, R.D., Lorrie Hulston, Natalie E. King, Rebecca W. Mohr, Leigh Mullinax (intern), Jan A. Smith, Kate M. Wheeler, R.D.**

Vice President, Editor-In-Chief, Oxmoor House: **Nancy Fitzpatrick Wyatt**
Senior Foods Editor, Oxmoor House: **Katherine M. Eakin**
Senior Editor, Copy and Homes, Oxmoor House: **Olivia Kindig Wells**
Art Director, Oxmoor House: **James Boone**

Director of Partnerships: **Betsey Hummel**
Vice President, Production and Distribution: **Phillip Lee**
Production Manager: **Greg Amason**
Production Assistant: **Faye Porter Bonner**

President and CEO: **Tom Angelillo**
Executive Vice Presidents: **Bruce Akin, Jeanetta Keller, Scott Sheppard**
Vice President, Administration: **Lane Schmitt**
Vice President, Corporate Marketing: **Greg Keyes**
Vice President, Consumer Marketing: **Pat Vander Meer**
Vice President, Finance: **Bruce Larson**
Vice President, Production: **Larry Rinehart**

Back cover: Turtle Cupcakes, page 86; photography by Brit Huckabay; styling by Virginia R. Cravens

WELCOME

One of our missions for *Day by Day* is to help make life easier for you, our reader. We know from experience and we hear from you that life can be overwhelming, with so many people and activities to schedule into already busy days.

Unfortunately, good eating habits sometimes move to the back burner. Worst-case scenarios: You either skip breakfast or gulp down a doughnut or a fast-food biscuit on the way to work; lunch hour turns into errand hour; and for dinner you grab a peanut butter-and-jelly sandwich because it's quick, cheap, and convenient. Or maybe you just eat the same foods day after day, week after week so you won't have to add meal-planning to your lengthy to-do list.

Of course, eating is necessary. But it doesn't have to be routine, and it definitely shouldn't be an afterthought. We'd like to help you rediscover the lost art of preparing meals. If you want to eat more regular, balanced meals or expand your scope of meal possibilities, this cookbook is for you. This selection of recipes will help you stay on track one meal at a time, one day at a time. Each recipe includes ***POINTS®,*** the basis for the Weight Watchers 1•2•3 Success® Weight Loss Plan. We also counted the calories, protein, fat, carbohydrates, fiber, cholesterol, iron, sodium, and calcium and included diabetic exchanges. To take some of the guesswork out of planning meals, we've organized the recipes into Breakfast, Lunch, Dinner, and Dessert chapters. And to make meal-planning even easier, we've provided sample menus to get you started (see page 92).

Eating regular meals and a variety of foods is at the foundation of a healthful diet. We hope these recipes will inspire you to return to the kitchen so you can enjoy homemade flavor whether you're at your table, at your desk, or on the run.

Alyson M. Haynes

day *by* day

c o n t e n t s

Out of Bed, Sleepyhead

THESE BREAKFAST IDEAS ARE
SOMETHING TO WAKE UP FOR.

You know that a well-balanced breakfast is important. But to serve milk, orange juice, biscuits, and eggs on weekdays would require time that you would rather spend sleeping. So how can you give breakfast the attention it deserves and yourself the nourishment you need?

In this chapter, we suggest healthful versions of your favorites, as well as dishes made with fruits and vegetables, low-fat dairy products, and whole grains which are part of a balanced diet.

We kept in mind your busy schedule; many of these recipes are quick and easy. Some you can make in advance, and then serve when you're in a rush—like when you've slept "just five more minutes."

The texture of English Muffin Bread provides plentiful pockets for butter or jam.

English Muffin Bread

3½ to 3¾ cups all-purpose flour, divided
1   cup whole wheat flour
½   cup oat bran
2   teaspoons salt
1   package rapid-rise yeast
1   cup very warm fat-free milk (120° to 130°)
1   cup very warm water (120° to 130°)
3   tablespoons reduced-calorie stick margarine, melted
Cooking spray
2   tablespoons cornmeal (not self-rising or cornmeal mix)

1. Combine 1½ cups all-purpose flour and next 4 ingredients in a large bowl; stir well. Add milk, water, and margarine; beat at medium speed of a mixer 2 minutes. Gradually stir in 2 cups all-purpose flour. Turn dough out onto a lightly floured surface; if dough is sticky, knead in remaining ½ cup flour. Cover dough with a large bowl; let rest 10 minutes.

2. Coat 2 (8½- x 4½-inch) loaf pans with cooking spray; sprinkle evenly with cornmeal. Divide dough in half; shape each portion into a loaf, and place in pans.

3. Cover and let rise in a warm place (85°), free from drafts, 1 hour or until doubled in bulk.

4. Preheat oven to 400°.

5. Bake at 400° for 25 minutes. Remove from pans immediately, and let cool on wire racks. Yield: 2 loaves, 24 servings (serving size: 1 slice).

POINTS: 2; **Diabetic Exchanges:** 1½ Starch
Per serving: CAL 112 (17% from fat); PRO 4g; FAT 2g (sat 0.1g); CARB 21g; FIB 1.5g; CHOL 0mg; IRON 1.3mg; SOD 210mg; CALC 19mg

Eggs Florentine

1   (10-ounce) package frozen leaf spinach
6   (¼-inch-thick) slices tomato
3   (2-ounce) whole wheat English muffins, split and toasted
6   large eggs, poached
Tarragon Sauce
Paprika (optional)

1. Cook spinach according to package directions, omitting salt; drain well.

2. Place 1 tomato slice on each muffin half. Divide spinach evenly among tomato slices; top each with an egg and 2 tablespoons Tarragon Sauce. Sprinkle with paprika, if desired. Yield: 6 servings.

POINTS: 4; **Diabetic Exchanges:** 1 Starch, 1 Veg, 1 L Meat, 1 Fat
Per serving: CAL 194 (32% from fat); PRO 11g; FAT 7g (sat 1.8g); CARB 22g; FIB 3.8g; CHOL 221mg; IRON 2.6mg; SOD 344mg; CALC 168mg

Tarragon Sauce:

½   cup light mayonnaise
3   tablespoons water
2   to 3 teaspoons fresh lemon juice
1   teaspoon prepared mustard
¼   teaspoon dried tarragon
⅛   teaspoon white pepper

1. Combine all ingredients in a small saucepan; stir until well blended. Place over low heat, and cook 3 minutes or until thoroughly heated, stirring constantly with a whisk (do not boil). Yield: ¾ cup.

Breakfast Burritos

Butter-flavored cooking spray
½   cup frozen chopped onion, celery, bell pepper, and parsley blend (such as McKenzie's seasoning blend), thawed
1   cup egg substitute
¼   teaspoon ground cumin
Dash of ground red pepper
4   (7-inch) flour tortillas
¼   cup (1 ounce) shredded reduced-fat sharp cheddar cheese
¼   cup salsa

1. Coat a medium nonstick skillet with cooking spray; place over medium-high heat until hot. Add seasoning blend; sauté 3 minutes. Reduce heat to medium. Stir in egg substitute, cumin, and ground red pepper; cook until egg is set, stirring occasionally.

2. Heat tortillas according to package directions. Spoon egg mixture evenly down centers of tortillas; sprinkle evenly with cheese. Roll up tortillas; top evenly with salsa. Yield: 4 servings.

POINTS: 3; **Diabetic Exchanges:** 1½ Starch, 1 L Meat
Per serving: CAL 168 (21% from fat); PRO 11g; FAT 4g (sat 1.2g); CARB 22g; FIB 1.6g; CHOL 5mg; IRON 2.2mg; SOD 381mg; CALC 129mg

Buckwheat-Cinnamon Pancakes

½ cup all-purpose flour
½ cup buckwheat flour
1 tablespoon sugar
2 teaspoons baking powder
¾ teaspoon ground cinnamon
¼ teaspoon salt
1 cup fat-free milk
1 tablespoon vegetable oil
1 large egg

1. Combine first 6 ingredients in a bowl, and stir well. Combine milk, oil, and egg; stir well. Add milk mixture to flour mixture, stirring until blended.

2. Spoon about ⅓ cup batter for each pancake onto a hot nonstick griddle or nonstick skillet. Turn pancakes when tops are covered with bubbles and edges look cooked. Yield: 2 servings (serving size: 3 pancakes).

POINTS: 8; **Diabetic Exchanges:** 4 Starch, 1½ Fat
Per serving: CAL 385 (25% from fat); PRO 14.5g; FAT 10.9g (sat 2.4g); CARB 59.5g; FIB 4.1g; CHOL 113mg; IRON 3.9mg; SOD 878mg; CALC 462mg

Cheddar, Bacon, and Tomato Strata

3 hickory-smoked bacon slices
1 cup slivered onion
2 garlic cloves, minced
8 cups cubed Italian bread (about 14 ounces)
Cooking spray
2 cups (8 ounces) shredded reduced-fat sharp cheddar cheese, divided
3 large tomatoes, each seeded and cut into 4 (½-inch-thick) slices
2 cups fat-free milk
¼ cup thinly sliced fresh basil
¼ teaspoon salt
¼ teaspoon dried thyme
¼ teaspoon pepper
3 large eggs
3 large egg whites

1. Cook bacon in a large nonstick skillet over medium heat until crisp. Remove bacon from skillet; crumble and set aside. Add onion to bacon fat in skillet; sauté 4 minutes. Add garlic, and

sauté 1 minute. Remove skillet from heat; stir in crumbled bacon. Set aside.

2. Place half of bread cubes in a 13- x 9-inch baking dish coated with cooking spray; top with ⅔ cup cheese, half of onion mixture, and 6 tomato slices. Combine milk and next 6 ingredients; stir well with a whisk. Pour half of milk mixture over tomatoes. Top with remaining half of bread cubes, ⅔ cup cheese, remaining half of onion mixture, remaining 6 tomato slices, and remaining half of milk mixture. Cover and chill at least 1 hour or up to 24 hours.

3. Preheat oven to 325°.

4. Bake, uncovered, at 325° for 55 minutes. Sprinkle with remaining ⅔ cup cheese; bake an

Pure maple syrup and seasonal fruit complement Buckwheat-Cinnamon Pancakes.

Coffee Royale

dditional 5 minutes or until cheese melts. Let and 5 minutes before serving. Yield: 8 servings.

OINTS: 7; **Diabetic Exchanges**: 1½ Starch, 1 Sk Milk, 1 M-F leat, ½ Veg, ½ Fat
er serving: CAL 316 (28% from fat); PRO 19.6g; FAT 9.8g (sat .8g); CARB 37g; FIB 2.3g; CHOL 106mg; IRON 1.9mg; SOD 70mg; CALC 356mg

Cinnamon Rolls

One taste and you'll fall in love with these tender olls filled with cinnamon-sugar and raisins and lathered with sweet, sticky glaze. And the best part? They start with a packaged roll mix, so hey're quick and easy to make.

(16-ounce) box hot roll mix
cup very warm water (120° to 130°)
¼ cup granulated sugar
3 tablespoons reduced-calorie stick margarine, softened and divided
1 large egg, lightly beaten
2 tablespoons all-purpose flour, divided
⅓ cup granulated sugar
2 teaspoons ground cinnamon
¼ cup raisins
Cooking spray
¼ cup sifted powdered sugar
1 tablespoon fat-free milk

1. Place contents of roll mix box (flour mixture and yeast packet) in a large bowl. Add very warm water, ¼ cup granulated sugar, 1 tablespoon margarine, and egg, stirring until moist. Shape dough into a ball.

2. Sprinkle 1½ tablespoons flour evenly over work surface. Turn dough out onto floured surface; knead until smooth and elastic (about 5 minutes). Cover and let rest 5 minutes.

3. Sprinkle remaining 1½ teaspoons flour evenly over work surface. Roll dough into a 16- x 10-inch rectangle on floured surface; spread remaining 2 tablespoons margarine over dough to within ½-inch of edge. Combine ⅓ cup granulated sugar and cinnamon; sprinkle over dough. Sprinkle with raisins. Roll up dough, jelly-roll fashion, beginning at 1 long edge; pinch seam to seal. Cut roll into 16 (1-inch) slices; place 8 slices, cut sides down, into each of 2 (8-inch) round cake pans coated with cooking spray. Cover and

let rise in a warm place (85°), free from drafts, 30 minutes or until doubled in bulk.

4. Preheat oven to 375°.

5. Bake at 375° for 20 minutes or until rolls are golden. Combine powdered sugar and milk, and stir well. Spread glaze over warm rolls. Yield: 16 servings.

POINTS: 4; **Diabetic Exchanges:** 2 Starch, 1 Fat
Per serving: CAL 191 (16% from fat); PRO 3.8g; FAT 3.4g (sat 0.3g); CARB 36.7g; FIB 0.2g; CHOL 16mg; IRON 0.5mg; SOD 142mg; CALC 29mg

Coffee Royale

If you prefer a less-spirited beverage, omit the amaretto and increase the coffee to 3¼ cups.

1¼ cups 1% low-fat milk
1 tablespoon sugar
¼ teaspoon ground cinnamon
2¾ cups hot strong brewed coffee
½ cup amaretto (almond-flavored liqueur)
6 (3-inch) cinnamon sticks (optional)

1. Combine first 3 ingredients in a medium saucepan; stir well. Place over medium heat, and cook 2 minutes or until sugar dissolves, stirring frequently. Remove from heat; stir in coffee and amaretto. Pour into mugs; garnish with cinnamon sticks, if desired. Yield: 6 servings (serving size: ¾ cup).

POINTS: 2; **Diabetic Exchanges:** 1 Starch
Per serving: CAL 96 (6% from fat); PRO 1.8g; FAT 0.6g (sat 0.4g); CARB 10.9g; FIB 0g; CHOL 2mg; IRON 0.5mg; SOD 28mg; CALC 66mg

Mango Smoothie

1 cup peeled sliced mango, chilled
1 cup plain low-fat yogurt
¾ cup sliced banana
1 tablespoon honey
Ice cubes

1. Place first 4 ingredients in a blender; process until smooth. Add ice cubes to blender to bring mixture to 3½-cup level; process until smooth. Yield: 3 servings (serving size: about 1 cup).

POINTS: 4; **Diabetic Exchanges:** 3½ Fruit, ½ Sk Milk
Per serving: CAL 247 (8% from fat); PRO 6.1g; FAT 2.1g (sat 1.1g); CARB 56.1g; FIB 4.4g; CHOL 5mg; IRON 0.6mg; SOD 60mg; CALC 164mg

Ham-and-Hash Brown Casserole

3   tablespoons all-purpose flour
¾   teaspoon dry mustard
¼   teaspoon pepper
⅛   teaspoon salt
1¾ cups evaporated fat-free milk, divided
4   ounces light processed cheese (such as Velveeta Light), cubed
1   (8-ounce) carton fat-free sour cream
1⅔ cups chopped lean ham
1   (28-ounce) package frozen cubed hash browns with onions and bell peppers, thawed
Cooking spray

1. Preheat oven to 350°.

2. Place first 4 ingredients in a medium saucepan; gradually add ½ cup milk, stirring with a whisk until well blended. Stir in remaining 1¼ cups milk. Place over medium heat, and cook until thick and bubbly, stirring constantly. Remove from heat; add cheese, stirring until cheese melts. Stir in sour cream.

3. Combine cheese sauce, ham, and hash brown in a large bowl; stir well. Spoon mixture into a 11- x 7-inch baking dish coated with cooking spray. Cover and bake at 350° for 30 minutes. Uncover and bake an additional 35 minutes or until golden. Yield: 8 servings.

POINTS: 5; **Diabetic Exchanges:** 2 Starch, 1 L Meat, ½ Fat
Per serving: CAL 238 (26% from fat); PRO 15g; FAT 7g (sat 2.7g); CARB 30g; FIB 0.6g; CHOL 24mg; IRON 1.7mg; SOD 749mg; CALC 250mg

Banana-Stuffed French Toast

1   cup mashed ripe banana
½   teaspoon lemon juice
4   (1-inch-thick) slices Italian bread
1   cup fat-free milk
2   tablespoons brown sugar
2   teaspoons vanilla extract
½   teaspoon ground cinnamon
¼   teaspoon baking powder
4   large egg whites
2   large eggs
2   teaspoons stick margarine, divided
½   cup pure maple syrup

1. Combine banana and juice in a bowl; stir well, and set aside. Cut bread slices in half crosswise; cut a slit through cut sides of each piece of bread to form a pocket. Stuff 2 tablespoons banana mixture into pocket of each piece of bread.

2. Combine milk and next 6 ingredients in a large shallow dish; stir well with a whisk. Arrange stuffed bread pieces in a single layer in dish, turning to coat. Cover and chill 45 minutes or until milk mixture is absorbed, turning bread pieces over after 20 minutes.

3. Melt 1 teaspoon margarine in a large nonstick skillet over medium heat. Add half of bread pieces; cook 4 minutes. Carefully turn bread over; cook 3 minutes or until browned. Repeat procedure with remaining margarine and bread pieces. Serve with syrup. Yield: 4 servings (serving size: 2 bread pieces and 2 tablespoons syrup).

POINTS: 7; **Diabetic Exchanges:** 4½ Starch
Per serving: CAL 354 (13% from fat); PRO 12g; FAT 5g (sat 1.3g); CARB 64.9g; FIB 2.5g; CHOL 108mg; IRON 1.9mg; SOD 321mg; CALC 144mg

Pair Ham-and-Hash Brown Casserole with sliced tomato and toast for a hearty, country-style breakfast.

Marmalade-Broiled Grapefruit

2   medium grapefruit
4   teaspoons orange marmalade
4   teaspoons brown sugar

1. Cut each grapefruit in half crosswise; remove seeds, and loosen sections of grapefruit with a knife.

2. Spread marmalade evenly over cut sides of grapefruit; sprinkle evenly with brown sugar. Broil 5 minutes or until hot and bubbly. Yield: 4 servings.

POINTS: 1; **Diabetic Exchanges:** 1 Fruit
Per serving: CAL 69 (1% from fat); PRO 0.8g; FAT 0.1g (sat 0g); CARB 17.7g; FIB 1.4g; CHOL 0mg; IRON 0.2mg; SOD 5mg; CALC 69mg

Prune Breakfast Butter

1¾ cups boiling water
2   regular-size Earl Grey tea bags
1   cup pitted prunes (about 8 ounces)
⅓ cup sugar
1   teaspoon grated lemon rind
½ teaspoon vanilla extract

1. Combine boiling water and tea bags in a medium bowl; cover and steep 5 minutes. Discard tea bags.

2. Combine brewed tea and prunes in a large saucepan; bring to a boil. Cover, reduce heat, and simmer 5 minutes or until prunes are tender. Remove from heat; let cool slightly. Place prune mixture in a blender; process until smooth.

Marmalade-Broiled Grapefruit can also be served as a fruit side dish with grilled pork chops.

3. Combine prune mixture, sugar, and lemon rind in pan; bring to a boil. Reduce heat, and simmer, uncovered, 20 minutes or until mixture is thick, stirring frequently. Remove from heat; stir in vanilla. Let cool. Store in an airtight container in refrigerator up to 2 months. Yield: 1¾ cups (serving size: 1 tablespoon).

POINTS: 0; **Diabetic Exchanges:** 1 Fruit
Per serving: CAL 29 (0% from fat); PRO 0.2g; FAT 0g; CARB 7.8g; FIB 0.6g; CHOL 0mg; IRON 0.2mg; SOD 0mg; CALC 4mg

Poached Fruit

2¾ cups apple juice
1½ tablespoons lemon juice
6 whole cloves
2 (3-inch) cinnamon sticks
¾ cup pitted prunes
¾ cup dried apricots
1½ cups peeled diced Granny Smith apple
1½ tablespoons grated orange rind
1 (8-ounce) carton vanilla low-fat yogurt
1 tablespoon reduced-calorie maple-flavored pancake syrup

1. Bring first 4 ingredients to a boil in a medium saucepan. Add prunes and apricots; cover, reduce heat, and simmer 15 minutes or until fruit is tender. Add apple and orange rind; simmer 5 minutes. Discard cloves and cinnamon sticks.

2. Combine yogurt and syrup in a bowl; stir well. Spoon poached fruit into bowls; top with yogurt mixture. Yield: 7 servings (serving size: ½ cup fruit and about 2 tablespoons yogurt mixture).

POINTS: 4; **Diabetic Exchanges:** 4 Fruit
Per serving: CAL 236 (6% from fat); PRO 3.5g; FAT 1.6g (sat 0.4g); CARB 57.1g; FIB 3.5g; CHOL 2mg; IRON 2.2mg; SOD 45mg; CALC 100mg

Mexican-Style Poached Eggs

4 (6-inch) corn tortillas
Cooking spray
¼ teaspoon garlic powder
¼ teaspoon ground cumin
1 (16-ounce) can red beans, rinsed and drained
1 (14½-ounce) can Mexican-style stewed tomatoes with garlic, cumin, and jalapeños, undrained
4 large eggs
2 tablespoons sliced green onions
¼ cup salsa
¼ cup fat-free sour cream
Chopped fresh cilantro (optional)

1. Preheat oven to 475°.

2. Coat both sides of tortillas with cooking spray. Combine garlic powder and cumin; sprinkle over 1 side of each tortilla. Stack tortillas, and cut stack into quarters. Place tortilla wedges in a single layer on a baking sheet; bake at 475° for 5 minutes or until crisp and golden, turning once.

3. Combine beans and tomatoes in a saucepan. Place over medium heat, and cook 10 minutes, stirring occasionally.

4. Add water to a large skillet to a depth of 2 inches; bring to a boil. Reduce heat, and simmer. Break 1 egg into a saucer; slip egg into simmering water, holding saucer as close as possible to water so egg yolk does not break. Repeat procedure with remaining 3 eggs. Simmer 5 minutes or until eggs are done; remove with a slotted spoon. Drain.

5. Spoon bean mixture evenly onto 4 plates; top each serving with 1½ teaspoons green onions, a poached egg, 1 tablespoon salsa, and 1 tablespoon sour cream. Sprinkle with cilantro, if desired. Divide tortilla wedges evenly among plates. Yield: 4 servings.

POINTS: 5; **Diabetic Exchanges:** 1 M-F Meat, 2 Starch, 1 Veg
Per serving: CAL 293; (22% from fat); PRO 17.7g; FAT 7.0g (sat 1.8g); CARB 40.8g; FIB 5.1g; CHOL 221mg; IRON 4.3mg; SOD 483mg; CALC 140mg

Crustless Grits-and-Ham Pie

1 cup water
⅓ cup uncooked quick-cooking grits
1 cup evaporated fat-free milk
¾ cup (3 ounces) shredded reduced-fat cheddar cheese
¾ cup chopped lean ham
1 tablespoon chopped fresh parsley
½ teaspoon dry mustard
½ teaspoon hot sauce
¼ teaspoon salt
3 large eggs, lightly beaten
Cooking spray

1. Preheat oven to 350°.

2. Bring 1 cup water to a boil in a small saucepan;

Breakfast Pizza

tir in grits. Cover, reduce heat, and simmer 4 minutes or until slightly thick.

5. Combine cooked grits, milk, and next 7 ingredients in a bowl; stir well. Pour into a 9-inch pie plate coated with cooking spray.

6. Bake at 350° for 30 minutes or until set. Let stand 5 minutes before serving. Cut into wedges. Yield: 6 servings.

POINTS: 4; **Diabetic Exchanges:** 1 M-F Meat, ½ Sk Milk, ½ Starch
Per serving: CAL 161 (36% from fat); PRO 13.4g; FAT 6.5g (sat 2.8g); CARB 13.3g; FIB 0g; CHOL 128mg; IRON 0.9mg; SOD 497mg; CALC 250mg

Breakfast Pizza

This recipe is sure to become a favorite.

¼ cup regular oats
1 teaspoon sugar
¼ teaspoon salt
1 package dry yeast
½ cup very warm water (120° to 130°)
1 tablespoon vegetable oil
⅓ cup whole wheat flour
⅓ cup all-purpose flour
Cooking spray
8 ounces turkey Italian sausage
1 cup (4 ounces) shredded reduced-fat sharp cheddar cheese
1 cup (4 ounces) shredded part-skim mozzarella cheese
1½ cups egg substitute
½ cup fat-free milk
¼ teaspoon dried oregano
⅛ to ¼ teaspoon freshly ground pepper
Oregano sprigs (optional)

1. Place oats in a blender or food processor; process until oats resemble flour.

2. Combine oat flour, sugar, salt, and yeast in a large bowl; stir well. Add very warm water and oil; stir well. Add whole wheat and all-purpose flours, stirring until blended.

3. Turn dough out onto a lightly floured surface, and knead until smooth and elastic (about 5 minutes). Place dough in a large bowl coated with cooking spray, turning to coat top. Cover and let rise in a warm place (85°), free from drafts, 1 hour or until doubled in bulk. Punch dough down, and turn out onto a lightly floured surface.

Roll dough to a 14-inch circle; place on a 12-inch pizza pan coated with cooking spray. Turn dough under to form a ½-inch-high rim.

4. Preheat oven to 425°.

5. Bake crust at 425° for 15 minutes. Remove crust from oven; set aside. Reduce oven temperature to 350°.

6. Remove casings from sausage. Cook sausage in a nonstick skillet over medium heat until browned, stirring to crumble; drain. Top pizza crust with sausage and cheeses. Combine egg substitute, milk, oregano, and pepper; stir well. Pour egg mixture evenly over sausage mixture. Bake at 350° for 30 minutes or until set. Garnish with oregano sprigs, if desired. Yield: 8 servings.

POINTS: 5; **Diabetic Exchanges:** 2½ L Meat, 1 Starch, ½ Fat
Per serving: CAL 235 (37% from fat); PRO 21g; FAT 9.6g (sat 3.9g); CARB 16g; FIB 1.8g; CHOL 32mg; IRON 1.9mg; SOD 639mg; CALC 238mg

Canadian Bacon With Currant Glaze

1 tablespoon brown sugar
1 teaspoon cornstarch
Dash of ground nutmeg
½ cup orange juice
2 tablespoons dried currants
1 (6-ounce) package lean Canadian bacon

1. Combine first 3 ingredients in a 2-cup glass measure or bowl. Gradually add orange juice, stirring with a whisk until blended. Add currants; microwave at HIGH 2 to 3 minutes or until slightly thick, stirring after 1½ minutes. Set aside. Arrange bacon slices, overlapping, in a circular pattern in bottom of a 9-inch pie plate. Pour orange juice mixture over bacon. Cover with wax paper, and microwave at HIGH 1½ to 2 minutes or until bacon is thoroughly heated, rotating pie plate a quarter-turn after 1 minute. Yield: 5 servings (servings size: 2 slices bacon and 1 tablespoon currant glaze).

POINTS: 2; **Diabetic Exchanges:** 1 L Meat, ½ Starch
Per serving: CAL 84 (27% from fat); PRO 7.3g; FAT 2.5g (sat 1g); CARB 7.9g; FIB 0.1g; CHOL 17mg; IRON 0.4mg; SOD 481mg; CALC 10mg

spray; top with half of apple mixture. Pour remaining batter into pan; top with remaining apple mixture, and sprinkle with brown sugar.

5. Bake at 350° for 1 hour and 10 minutes or until a wooden pick inserted in center comes out clean. Let cool in pan 10 minutes; remove from pan, and let cool on a wire rack. Yield: 16 servings.

POINTS: 4; Diabetic Exchanges: 2½ Starch, ½ Fat
Per serving: CAL 206 (26% from fat); PRO 3.3g; FAT 6g (sat 1.2g); CARB 35.2g; FIB 0.8g; CHOL 0mg; IRON 1.9mg; SOD 191mg; CALC 55mg

Garlic-Cheese Grits

4 cups water
½ teaspoon salt
2 large garlic cloves, minced
1 cup uncooked quick-cooking grits
6 ounces light processed cheese (such as Velveeta Light), cubed
½ teaspoon Worcestershire sauce
¼ teaspoon dry mustard
⅛ teaspoon ground red pepper

1. Bring first 3 ingredients to a boil in a medium saucepan. Stir in grits; cover, reduce heat, and simmer 5 minutes, stirring frequently. Add cheese and remaining ingredients; cook 1 minute or until cheese melts, stirring constantly. Yield: 6 servings (serving size: ¾ cup).

POINTS: 3; Diabetic Exchanges: ½ M-F Meat, 1½ Starch
Per serving: CAL 142 (13% from fat); PRO 9.3g; FAT 2.2g (sat 0.6g); CARB 21.4g; FIB 1.3g; CHOL 0mg; IRON 0.9mg; SOD 608mg; CALC 201mg

Glazed Cinnamon-Orange Biscuits

1½ cups sifted powdered sugar
2 tablespoons water
½ teaspoon orange extract
¼ teaspoon vanilla extract
3½ cups reduced-fat biscuit and baking mix (such as Bisquick)
3 tablespoons granulated sugar
3 tablespoons orange drink mix (such as Tang)
2½ teaspoons ground cinnamon
1¼ cups fat-free milk
Cooking spray

1. Preheat oven to 425°.

2. Combine first 4 ingredients in a small bowl;

Our test kitchens preferred Rome and Granny Smith apples in Fresh Apple Coffee Cake, but any cooking apple will do.

Fresh Apple Coffee Cake

4 cups unpeeled, finely chopped cooking apple
½ cup orange juice, divided
1½ teaspoons ground cinnamon
1 cup sugar
½ cup stick margarine, softened
1 cup egg substitute
¼ cup fat-free milk
3 cups sifted cake flour
2 teaspoons baking powder
¼ teaspoon salt
2½ teaspoons vanilla extract
Cooking spray
2 tablespoons brown sugar

1. Preheat oven to 350°.

2. Combine apple, ¼ cup orange juice, and cinnamon in a bowl; stir well, and set aside.

3. Cream sugar and margarine at medium speed of a mixer until light and fluffy (about 5 minutes). Add egg substitute; beat 4 minutes at medium speed or until well blended.

4. Combine remaining ¼ cup orange juice and milk; set aside. Combine flour, baking powder, and salt. With mixer running at low speed, add flour mixture to creamed mixture alternately with milk mixture, beginning and ending with flour mixture. Stir in vanilla. Pour half of batter into a 10-inch tube pan coated with cooking

tir until well blended. Set glaze aside.

3. Combine biscuit and baking mix and next 3 ingredients in a bowl; make a well in center of mixture. Add milk, stirring until moist.

4. Drop dough by heaping tablespoons 1½ inches apart onto baking sheets coated with cooking spray. Bake at 425° for 6 minutes or until bottoms are lightly browned. Remove biscuits from oven; drizzle glaze evenly over biscuits. Serve warm. Yield: 2½ dozen (serving size: 1 biscuit).

POINTS: 2; **Diabetic Exchanges:** 1½ Starch
Per serving: CAL 117 (8% from fat); PRO 1.8g; FAT 1.1g (sat 0.3g); CARB 24.8g; FIB 0.3g; CHOL 0mg; IRON 0.7mg; SOD 208mg; CALC 41mg

Spicy Sausage

1 pound lean ground pork
1 teaspoon rubbed sage
½ teaspoon freshly ground pepper
¼ to ½ teaspoon garlic powder
¼ teaspoon onion powder
¼ teaspoon ground mace
¼ teaspoon salt
¼ teaspoon ground allspice
Dash of ground cloves
Cooking spray

1. Combine all ingredients except cooking spray in a large bowl; stir well. Shape into 6 (¾-inch-thick) patties. Coat a large nonstick skillet with cooking spray; place over medium heat until hot. Add patties; cook 7 minutes on each side or until browned and done. Yield: 6 servings.

POINTS: 2; **Diabetic Exchanges:** 2 L Meat
Per serving: CAL 105 (34% from fat); PRO 20g; FAT 4g (sat 2g); CARB 0.5g; FIB 0.1g; CHOL 72mg; IRON 0.9mg; SOD 95mg; CALC 9mg

Eggs Benedict

6 (⅔-ounce) slices lean Canadian bacon
Cooking spray
3 (2-ounce) whole wheat English muffins, split and toasted
6 large eggs, poached
Mock Hollandaise Sauce

1. Place bacon in a large nonstick skillet coated with cooking spray; cook over medium heat until thoroughly heated, turning once.

2. Place 1 bacon slice on each muffin half. Top each with a poached egg and 2 tablespoons Mock Hollandaise Sauce. Serve immediately. Yield: 6 servings.

POINTS: 3; **Diabetic Exchanges:** 1 Starch, 1 M-F Meat
Per serving: CAL 156 (35% from fat); PRO 11g; FAT 6g (sat 1.5g); CARB 16g; FIB 2.2g; CHOL 155mg; IRON 1.4mg; SOD 563mg; CALC 162mg

Mock Hollandaise Sauce:

¾ cup plain low-fat yogurt, divided
1 large egg yolk
1 tablespoon fresh lemon juice
¼ teaspoon salt
⅛ teaspoon dry mustard

1. Combine ¼ cup yogurt and egg yolk in a small saucepan; stir well. Place over low heat, and cook 6 minutes or until thick, stirring constantly with a whisk (do not boil). Stir in remaining ½ cup yogurt, lemon juice, salt, and mustard; cook until thoroughly heated (do not boil). Yield: ¾ cup.

Spicy Sausage provides all the flavor of regular sausage with half the fat.

Bran Muffins

Bran Muffins

Since the batter keeps in the refrigerator all week, you can enjoy freshly baked muffins each morning. Bake them one at a time or by the batch.

3   cups shreds of wheat bran cereal (such as All Bran)
1   cup boiling water
¾   cup raisins
2⅓ cups all-purpose flour
¾   cup sugar
2   teaspoons baking soda
½   teaspoon salt
2   cups low-fat buttermilk
¼   cup plus 2 tablespoons vegetable oil
2   large eggs
Cooking spray

1. Preheat oven to 350°.

2. Combine first 3 ingredients in a bowl; stir well. Cover and let stand 10 minutes.

3. Combine flour and next 3 ingredients in a large bowl, and stir well; make a well in center of mixture. Combine buttermilk, oil, and eggs in a bowl; stir well with a whisk. Add cereal mixture and buttermilk mixture to flour mixture, stirring just until moist.

4. Divide batter evenly among muffin cups coated with cooking spray. Bake at 350° for 22 minutes or until a wooden pick inserted in center comes out clean. Remove from pans immediately; place on a wire rack. Yield: 2 dozen muffins (serving size: 1 muffin).

Note: Store muffin batter in an airtight container in refrigerator for up to 1 week, if desired.

POINTS: 3; Diabetic Exchanges: 2 Starch
Per serving: CAL 157 (27% from fat); PRO 4.1g; FAT 4.7g (sat 0.8g); CARB 27.9g; FIB 4g; CHOL 18mg; IRON 2.3mg; SOD 270mg; CALC 67mg

Sausage Breakfast Casserole

3   cups (1-inch) cubed French bread
Cooking spray
½   pound bulk turkey breakfast sausage
¼   cup chopped green onions
¾   cup (3 ounces) shredded reduced-fat sharp cheddar cheese
1   cup fat-free milk
1   cup egg substitute

½   teaspoon dry mustard
¼   teaspoon salt
¼   teaspoon pepper

1. Place bread cubes in an 11- x 7-inch baking dish coated with cooking spray.

2. Coat a large nonstick skillet with cooking spray; place over medium-high heat until hot. Add sausage and green onions; cook until sausage is browned, stirring to crumble. Drain. Spoon sausage mixture over bread cubes; top bread cubes with cheese.

3. Combine milk and next 4 ingredients; stir well. Pour milk mixture over bread mixture, pressing down on bread mixture with a spatula to soak bread. Cover casserole, and chill 8 hours or overnight.

4. Preheat oven to 350°.

5. Bake, uncovered, at 350° for 30 minutes or until set and lightly browned. Let stand 5 minutes before serving. Yield: 6 servings.

POINTS: 3; Diabetic Exchanges: 1½ L Meat, 1 Starch
Per serving: CAL 156 (25% from fat); PRO 13g; FAT 4.4g (sat 1.9g); CARB 15.7g; FIB 0.5g; CHOL 16mg; IRON 1.3mg; SOD 450mg; CALC 205mg

Spicy Virgin Mary

1   (46-ounce) can reduced-salt tomato juice
1   (14½-ounce) can beef broth
¼   cup low-salt Worcestershire sauce
3   tablespoons fresh lime juice
1½ teaspoons seasoned salt
1   teaspoon celery seeds
½   teaspoon onion powder
½   teaspoon freshly ground pepper
¼   teaspoon hot sauce
⅛   teaspoon garlic powder
Ice cubes
Celery stalks (optional)

1. Combine first 10 ingredients in a pitcher; stir well. Cover and chill. Serve over ice; garnish with celery stalks, if desired. Yield: 8 servings (serving size: about 1 cup).

POINTS: 1; Diabetic Exchanges: 2 Veg
Per serving: CAL 49 (1% from fat); PRO 1.9g; FAT 0.1g (sat 0g); CARB 11.4g; FIB 0.1g; CHOL 0mg; IRON 1mg; SOD 612mg; CALC 6mg

- If you grease more muffin cups than you need, fill the empty cups with water to keep the grease from baking onto the cups.

- The secret of good muffins is in the mixing. Combine all the dry ingredients in a bowl, and form a well in the center of the mixture. Add the liquid ingredients all at once, and stir only enough to moisten the dry ingredients. The mixture will be lumpy, but further mixing will make the muffins tough.

- When preparing a recipe that calls for all-purpose or whole wheat flour, it isn't necessary to sift the flour; simply stir before measuring.

- Unless otherwise specified, always preheat the oven at least 20 minutes before baking.

- If the muffins are done ahead of serving time, loosen them from their cups, tilt slightly, and slide the pan back into the oven to stay warm (oven should be off). This lets the extra moisture escape and prevents a soggy bottom.

Applesauce Oatmeal

1   cup fat-free milk
¾   cup regular oats
½   cup unsweetened applesauce
1   tablespoon brown sugar
⅛   teaspoon vanilla extract
Dash of ground cinnamon

1. Place milk in a small saucepan; bring to a boil over medium heat. Add oats, and cook 8 minutes or until thick, stirring occasionally. Add applesauce, brown sugar, vanilla, and cinnamon; cook 1 minute or until thoroughly heated, stirring occasionally. Yield: 2 servings (serving size: about ¾ cup).

POINTS: 3; **Diabetic Exchanges:** 2 Starch, ½ Sk Milk
Per serving: CAL 179 (8% from fat); PRO 7.5g; FAT 1.5g (sat 0.4g); CARB 33.7g; FIB 2.6g; CHOL 2mg; IRON 1.1mg; SOD 67mg; CALC 170mg

Brunch Ambrosia

3½ cups sliced Fuji or Gala apple (about 2)
2¼ cups pink grapefruit sections (about 2)
1   cup orange sections (about 2)
½   cup orange juice
2   tablespoons flaked sweetened coconut

1. Combine apple, grapefruit, orange, and orange juice in a bowl; toss gently. Cover and chill 1 hour. Spoon fruit into bowls, and sprinkle with coconut. Yield: 6 servings (serving size: 1 cup fruit mixture and 1 teaspoon coconut).

POINTS: 1; **Diabetic Exchanges:** 1½ Fruit
Per serving: CAL 94 (10% from fat); PRO 1.2g; FAT 1g (sat 0.7g); CARB 22.2g; FIB 4.2g; CHOL 0mg; IRON 0.3mg; SOD 5mg; CALC 33mg

Cheddar-Vegetable Omelet

Cooking spray
1   cup chopped green bell pepper
½   cup sliced fresh mushrooms
1   cup peeled diced tomato
2   large eggs
2   large egg whites
¼   cup fat-free milk
2   tablespoons picante sauce
½   teaspoon salt
Dash of pepper
¼   cup (1 ounce) shredded reduced-fat sharp
      cheddar cheese

1. Coat a large nonstick skillet with cooking spray, and place over medium heat until hot. Add bell pepper and mushrooms; sauté 3 minutes or until tender. Stir in tomato; cook just until thoroughly heated. Remove from skillet; set aside, and keep warm.

2. Combine eggs, egg whites, and next 4 ingredients in a bowl; stir well with a whisk. Recoat skillet with cooking spray, and place over medium-low heat until hot. Add egg mixture; cook until center is set (do not stir).

3. Spoon vegetable mixture over half of omelet; sprinkle with cheese. Loosen omelet with a spatula, and fold omelet in half. Cut omelet in half. Yield: 2 servings (serving size: ½ omelet).

POINTS: 4; **Diabetic Exchanges:** 2 Veg, 2 L Meat, ½ Fat
Per serving: CAL 179 (42% from fat); PRO 16.5g; FAT 8.4g (sat 3.3g); CARB 9.5g; FIB 1.5g; CHOL 231mg; IRON 1.9mg; SOD 997mg; CALC 187mg

Buttermilk Waffles

4   cups self-rising flour
2   tablespoons sugar
¼   teaspoon baking soda
4   cups low-fat buttermilk
½   cup vegetable oil
8   large egg whites
Cooking spray

1. Combine flour, sugar, and baking soda in a large bowl. Combine buttermilk and oil; stir well. Add buttermilk mixture to flour mixture, stirring just until moist.

2. Beat egg whites at high speed of a mixer until stiff peaks form. Stir one-fourth of egg whites into batter; fold remaining egg whites into batter.

3. Preheat waffle iron, and coat with cooking spray. Spoon about ¼ cup batter per 4-inch waffle onto hot waffle iron, spreading batter to edges. Cook until steaming stops; repeat procedure with remaining batter. Yield: 16 servings (serving size: 2 waffles).

POINTS: 5; **Diabetic Exchanges:** 2 Starch, 1 Fat
Per serving: CAL 105 (33% from fat); PRO 7.2g; FAT 8.1g (sat 1.3g); CARB 28.6g; FIB 0.8g; CHOL 0mg; IRON 1.5mg; SOD 78mg; CALC 81mg

Applesauce Oatmeal

Drop Biscuits With Sausage Gravy

Drop Biscuits With Sausage Gravy

The perfect breakfast—as any true Southerner would attest—is a biscuit smothered with creamy sausage gravy. Here's a version you can enjoy—without all the fat.

1 cup all-purpose flour
1½ teaspoons baking powder
⅛ teaspoon salt
½ cup fat-free milk
1 teaspoon stick margarine, melted
Butter-flavored cooking spray
Sausage Gravy
Additional freshly ground pepper (optional)

1. Preheat oven to 450°.

2. Combine first 3 ingredients in a bowl; stir well, and make a well in center of mixture. Combine milk and margarine; add to flour mixture, stirring just until moist.

3. Drop batter by heaping tablespoons onto a baking sheet coated with cooking spray. Coat biscuits with cooking spray. Bake at 450° for 11 minutes or until golden. Split biscuits, and top with Sausage Gravy. Sprinkle with additional pepper, if desired. Yield: 6 servings (serving size: 1 biscuit and about ⅓ cup gravy).

POINTS: 4; **Diabetic Exchanges:** 1½ Starch, 1½ L Meat
Per serving: CAL 199 (19% from fat); PRO 14.7g; FAT 4.2g (sat 1g); CARB 24.6g; FIB 0.7g; CHOL 27mg; IRON 1.8mg; SOD 271mg; CALC 197mg

Sausage Gravy:

½ pound turkey breakfast sausage links
1 tablespoon stick margarine
3 tablespoons all-purpose flour
2¼ cups fat-free milk
½ teaspoon freshly ground pepper
⅛ teaspoon salt

1. Remove casings from sausage. Melt margarine in a medium saucepan over medium heat. Add sausage, and cook until browned, stirring to crumble. Sprinkle flour over sausage, and cook 1 minute, stirring constantly. Gradually add milk, stirring until well blended. Cook 8 minutes or until thick, stirring constantly. Remove from heat; stir in pepper and salt. Yield: about 2 cups.

Honey Pancakes

3 cups all-purpose flour
2 tablespoons baking powder
½ teaspoon salt
3 cups fat-free milk
½ cup egg substitute
¼ cup vegetable oil
¼ cup honey

1. Combine first 3 ingredients in a large bowl, and stir well. Combine milk and next 3 ingredients; stir well. Add milk mixture to flour mixture, stirring until blended.

2. Spoon about ¼ cup batter for each pancake onto a hot nonstick griddle or nonstick skillet. Turn pancakes when tops are covered with bubbles and edges look cooked. Yield 14 servings (serving size: 2 pancakes).

Note: These pancakes freeze well. Place them in a single layer on a wax paper-lined baking sheet, and freeze. Place frozen pancakes in an airtight container, and return to freezer. To reheat frozen pancakes, microwave 1 pancake at HIGH 30 to 45 seconds; 2 pancakes at HIGH 1 minute to 1 minute and 10 seconds; 3 pancakes at HIGH 1 minute and 15 seconds to 1 minute and 30 seconds or until thoroughly heated.

POINTS: 4; **Diabetic Exchanges:** 2 Starch, ½ Fat
Per serving: CAL 173 (21% from fat); PRO 5g; FAT 4g (sat 0.8g); CARB 29g; FIB 0.7g; CHOL 1mg; IRON 1.6mg; SOD 334mg; CALC 188mg

COOKING PANCAKES:

When the top surface is full of bubbles, it's time to flip the pancakes.

Blueberry Muffins

1 cup all-purpose flour
¾ cup whole wheat flour
⅓ cup sugar
2 teaspoons baking powder
½ teaspoon ground cinnamon
¼ teaspoon salt
1 cup fresh or frozen blueberries, thawed and drained
¾ cup fat-free milk
¼ cup vegetable oil
1 teaspoon grated orange rind
1 teaspoon vanilla extract
2 large egg whites
Cooking spray

1. Preheat oven to 350°.

2. Combine flours, sugar, baking powder, cinnamon, and salt in a large bowl; stir well. Add blueberries, and toss gently to coat. Make a well in center of mixture.

3. Combine milk and next 4 ingredients; stir well. Add milk mixture to flour mixture, stirring just until moist. Divide batter evenly among muffin cups coated with cooking spray. Bake at 350° for 15 minutes or until done. Remove from pans immediately; place on a wire rack. Serve warm or at room temperature. Yield: 1 dozen (serving size: 1 muffin).

Note: You may freeze muffins in an airtight container. Then reheat frozen muffins by microwaving 1 muffin at HIGH 40 to 50 seconds; 2 muffins at HIGH 1 to 1½ minutes or until thoroughly heated.

POINTS: 3; **Diabetic Exchanges:** 1½ Starch, ½ Fat
Per serving: CAL 146 (31% from fat); PRO 3.3g; FAT 5.1g (sat 0.9g); CARB 21.9g; FIB 1.6g; CHOL 0mg; IRON 0.9mg; SOD 116mg; CALC 57mg

Open-Faced Apple-Cheese Bagels

Cooking spray
1 medium Granny Smith apple, cut into 16 wedges
1 teaspoon brown sugar
¼ cup light cream cheese, softened
2 (3-ounce) plain bagels, split and toasted (such as Lender's Big and Crusty)

2 (⅔-ounce) slices lean Canadian bacon, coarsely chopped
¼ cup (1 ounce) shredded reduced-fat sharp cheddar cheese
2 tablespoons chopped green onions

1. Preheat oven to 425°.

2. Coat a nonstick skillet with cooking spray; place over medium-high heat until hot. Add apple and brown sugar; sauté 3 minutes. Remove from heat; set aside.

3. Spread 1 tablespoon cream cheese over each bagel half; top each with 4 apple wedges. Sprinkle bacon and cheese over apple wedges. Bake at 425° for 8 minutes. Remove from oven; sprinkle with green onions. Yield: 4 servings (serving size: 1 bagel half).

POINTS: 4; **Diabetic Exchanges:** 2 Starch, ½ L Meat, ½ Fat
Per serving: CAL 212 (21% from fat); PRO 10g; FAT 5g (sat 2.5g); CARB 30g; FIB 2.1g; CHOL 18mg; IRON 1.8mg; SOD 508mg; CALC 120mg

Crunchy Granola

Coconut, almonds, and sunflower seeds abound in this no-oil recipe.

1 cup boiling water
½ cup sweetened dried cranberries (such as Craisins)
¼ cup firmly packed brown sugar
1 (6-ounce) bag dried mixed tropical fruit
3 cups regular oats
½ cup sliced almonds
½ cup roasted salted sunflower seeds
¼ cup flaked sweetened coconut
2 tablespoons fat-free dry milk
1 teaspoon ground cinnamon

1. Preheat oven to 300°.

2. Combine first 4 ingredients in a large bowl; let stand 15 minutes. Add oats and next 5 ingredients; stir well. Spread mixture evenly in a jelly-roll pan, and bake at 300° for 1 hour, stirring every 15 minutes. Let granola cool to room temperature. Store in an airtight container. Yield: 12 servings (serving size: ½ cup).

POINTS: 4; **Diabetic Exchanges:** 2 ½ Starch, 1 Fat
Per serving: CAL 224 (28% from fat); PRO 6.3g; FAT 7g (sat 1.4g); CARB 36.4g; FIB 3.4g; CHOL 0mg; IRON 2.2mg; SOD 19mg; CALC 58mg

Crunchy Granola

Bagels

agels

    package dry yeast
¾ cups warm water (105° to 115°)
    tablespoons honey
to 5½ cups bread flour, divided
    teaspoons salt
Cooking spray
½ cup sesame seeds or any mix of poppy
    seeds, caraway seeds, sea salt, or instant
    minced onion and dried garlic flakes
    tablespoon cornmeal

. Combine yeast and warm water in a bowl; let
tand 5 minutes. Stir in honey. Combine yeast
mixture, 2 cups flour, and salt in a large bowl;
eat at low speed of a heavy-duty stand mixer 4
minutes or until smooth.

2. Gradually stir in enough of remaining flour to
make a soft dough. Beat at medium-low speed
with a dough hook 8 minutes or until smooth
nd elastic. Divide dough into 12 equal portions;
oll each into a smooth ball. Cover and let rest 5
minutes.

3. Roll each ball into an 11-inch rope. Bring ends
of ropes together, and pinch to seal. Roll bagel
round palm of hand to make a ring. Place on
aking sheets coated with cooking spray; cover
nd chill 12 to 18 hours.

4. Bring 3½ quarts water to a boil in a large
Dutch oven. Add bagels, 4 at a time, and cook 30
econds, turning once. Remove bagels with a slot-
ed spoon; place on wire racks. Dredge bagels in

sesame seeds. Repeat procedure with remaining
bagels and sesame seeds.

5. Preheat oven to 450°.

6. Coat baking sheets with cooking spray, and
sprinkle with cornmeal. Place bagels on prepared
pans. Bake at 450° for 13 minutes or until
golden. Yield: 1 dozen (serving size: 1 bagel).

Note: To make Cinnamon-Raisin Bagels, stir 1
cup raisins and 2 teaspoons ground cinnamon
into dough before dividing dough into pieces.

POINTS: 5; **Diabetic Exchanges:** 3 Starch
Per serving: CAL 255 (15% from fat); PRO 8.5g; FAT 4.2g (sat
0.6g); CARB 48.6g; FIB 0.4g; CHOL 0mg; IRON 3.6mg; SOD
393mg; CALC 68mg

Bran-and-Fruit Muesli

2   cups wheat bran flakes cereal (such as Bran
     Flakes)
1½ cups toasted high-fiber corn cereal (such as
     Quaker Crunchy Corn Bran)
½   cup toasted wheat germ
⅓   cup chopped pitted dates
⅓   cup chopped dried apples
¼   cup chopped walnuts, toasted
¼   cup unsalted sunflower seeds, toasted
¼   cup dried banana chips, crushed

1. Combine all ingredients; stir well. Store in an
airtight container in a cool, dry place. Serve with
milk. Yield: 10 servings (serving size: ½ cup).

POINTS: 2; **Diabetic Exchanges:** 1½ Starch
Per serving: CAL 139 (30% from fat); PRO 4.8g; FAT 4.6g (sat
0.4g); CARB 23.2g; FIB 4g; CHOL 0mg; IRON 3.9mg; SOD 124mg;
CALC 22mg

STEP BY STEP TO BAGELS

1. Roll bagel on surface around palm of
hand to make a ring.

2. Boil bagels briefly in a large Dutch oven
to set the shape.

3. Dip bagels into sesame seeds. Place on
baking sheets coated with cooking spray
and sprinkled with cornmeal to bake.

It's in the Bag

LUNCH CAN BE THE KEY TO
A WELL-ROUNDED DIET.

If you're starving by noon or just in a hurry, you may grab a snack to tide you over or pick up fast food while you run errands. But lunch, like breakfast, is an integral part of a day's nutrition. Often, the foods you neglect at lunchtime are fruits and vegetables. In their place may be a burger and fries. With our make-ahead recipes, it's easy to choose healthy foods that help you budget your daily *POINTS* more efficiently.

Whether you're eating on the run or munching at your desk, a nutritious lunch requires a bit of planning ahead. These recipes can be prepared in advance, so they're ready when you are. With these lunch options in your arsenal of power foods, you can be sure you're doing your body a favor.

Quick-and-Hearty Minestrone has only five ingredients, aside from staples.

Pickled Carrots with a

ham sandwich

Quick-and-Hearty Minestrone

Two types of pasta—ditalini that we added and rotini from the soup mix—thicken this soup.

½ pound ground round
6 cups water
1 (14.5-ounce) can no-salt-added stewed tomatoes, undrained and chopped
1 (4.4-ounce) package minestrone soup mix (such as Lipton's Kettle Creations)
½ cup uncooked ditalini (very short tubular macaroni)
½ teaspoon pepper
¼ teaspoon salt
1 (10-ounce) package frozen chopped spinach, thawed, drained, and squeezed dry

1. Cook meat in a Dutch oven over medium heat until browned, stirring to crumble. Drain well, and return meat to pan. Stir in water, tomatoes, and soup mix; bring to a boil. Reduce heat, and simmer, uncovered, 10 minutes, stirring occasionally. Stir in ditalini, pepper, salt, and spinach; simmer 7 minutes or until pasta is done. Serve soup immediately or store in an airtight container in refrigerator. Yield: 4 servings (serving size: 2 cups).

Note: If Lipton's minestrone soup mix is not available in your area, you may order the product by calling 1-800-697-7887 or visiting Lipton's website at www.lipton.com/800/800.html.

POINTS: 5; **Diabetic Exchanges:** 2 Starch, 2 Veg, 2 V-L Meat
Per serving: CAL 281 (12% from fat); PRO 22g; FAT 3.7g (sat 0.9g); CARB 40.4g; FIB 5.6g; CHOL 32mg; IRON 4.9mg; SOD 998mg; CALC 129mg

Pickled Carrots

These zesty carrots are a tasty side dish for a sandwich or salad at lunch. To save time, purchase precut carrot sticks in a bag.

1½ cups cider vinegar
1½ cups water
1 cup sugar
2 pounds carrots, peeled and cut into sticks
2 tablespoons dill seeds
3 to 4 garlic cloves, peeled and halved

1. Combine first 3 ingredients in a large saucepan; bring to a boil, and cook until sugar dissolves, stirring constantly. Add carrot sticks, dill seeds, and garlic; return to a boil. Cover, reduce heat, and simmer 6 minutes. Remove from heat; let cool. Cover and chill at least 8 hours.

2. Drain carrots to serve; discard garlic, if desired. Yield: 5 servings (serving size: 1 cup).

POINTS: 2; **Diabetic Exchanges:** 2 Veg, ½ Starch
Per serving: CAL 83 (4% from fat); PRO 0.7g; FAT 0.4g (sat 0g); CARB 20.9g; FIB 0.1g; CHOL 0mg; IRON 0.1mg; SOD 5mg; CALC 5mg

Gazpacho

Gazpacho is a refreshing chilled Spanish soup that contains garden-fresh vegetables.

1 (10¾-ounce) can condensed tomato soup, undiluted
1½ cups tomato juice
1¼ cups water
½ cup chopped cucumber
½ cup chopped tomato
½ cup chopped green bell pepper
½ cup chopped onion
3 tablespoons fat-free Italian dressing
1 tablespoon lemon juice
¼ teaspoon pepper
¼ teaspoon hot sauce
1 garlic clove, minced

1. Combine all ingredients in a large bowl; stir well. Cover and chill at least 6 hours. Yield: 6 servings (serving size: about 1 cup).

POINTS: 1; **Diabetic Exchanges:** 2 Veg
Per serving: CAL 60 (14% from fat); PRO 1.4g; FAT 0.9g (sat 0.1g); CARB 10.3g; FIB 1.1g; CHOL 0mg; IRON 1mg; SOD 578mg; CALC 10mg

Fresh-Vegetable Soup

Make a big batch of this soup on Sunday when there's plenty of time to cut and chop all the vegetables. Then, during the week, dish up a bowl and reheat it for lunch in no time flat. Refrigerate the soup in an airtight container for up to 1 week, or freeze it for up to 3 months.

2 tablespoons olive oil
2 cups chopped onion
5 garlic cloves, minced
2 cups chopped celery
2 cups (2-inch) cut green beans (about ½ pound)
1½ cups fresh corn kernels (about 3 ears)
1 cup peeled thinly sliced carrot

1 medium zucchini, halved lengthwise and sliced (about 1 cup)
1 teaspoon dried basil
1 teaspoon dried oregano
1 teaspoon dried rosemary
4 (14¼-ounce) cans fat-free beef broth
1 (15-ounce) can kidney beans, drained
4 cups seeded chopped tomato
⅔ cup uncooked elbow macaroni
1 (8-ounce) can no-salt-added tomato sauce
2 cups thinly sliced green cabbage
¾ teaspoon salt
¾ teaspoon pepper
1 cup grated Parmesan cheese

1. Heat oil in a stockpot over medium-high heat. Add onion and garlic; sauté 2 minutes. Stir in celery and next 9 ingredients; bring to a boil. Cover, reduce heat, and simmer 30 minutes. Add tomato, macaroni, and tomato sauce; bring to a boil. Cover, reduce heat, and simmer 20 minutes or until pasta is done. Add cabbage, salt, and pepper; cook 5 minutes or until cabbage wilts. Ladle soup into bowls; top with cheese. Yield: 8 servings (serving size: 2 cups soup and 2 tablespoons cheese).

POINTS: 5; **Diabetic Exchanges:** 2 Starch, 2 Veg, 1 Fat, ½ V-L Meat
Per serving: CAL 272 (25% from fat); PRO 12.5g; FAT 7.6g (sat 2.6g); CARB 39.4g; FIB 6.4g; CHOL 8mg; IRON 3mg; SOD 529mg; CALC 213mg

Chicken Salad in Cantaloupe

Serve with assorted crackers.

3 cups shredded cooked chicken breast
1½ cups peeled cubed papaya
1 cup chopped red bell pepper
¼ cup minced fresh cilantro
3 tablespoons white balsamic vinegar
1½ tablespoons fresh lime juice
1½ tablespoons Dijon mustard
4 teaspoons honey
2 teaspoons olive oil
¼ teaspoon ground red pepper
2 small cantaloupes

1. Combine first 4 ingredients in a bowl; toss well. Combine vinegar and next 5 ingredients in a small bowl; stir well. Pour vinegar mixture over

chicken mixture; toss well. Cover and chill.

2. Cut each cantaloupe in half; discard seeds. Cu[t] a thin slice from bottom of each melon half s[o] that it will sit flat, if necessary. Spoon chicke[n] mixture evenly into melon halves. Serve immedi ately or wrap in plastic wrap and chill until read[y] to serve. Yield: 4 servings.

POINTS: 7; **Diabetic Exchanges:** 5 V-L Meat, 1 Starch, 1½ Fruit
Per serving: CAL 366 (19% from fat); PRO 38.4g; FAT 7.7g (sa[t] 1.9g); CARB 37.5g; FIB 3.4g; CHOL 96mg; IRON 2.2mg; SO[D] 281mg; CALC 63mg

Chilled Borscht

To peel beets after they've been cooked, gentl[y] rub the skin with your fingers. The skin shoul[d] come right off.

2 pounds large fresh beets
Butter-flavored cooking spray
1 teaspoon reduced-calorie stick margarine
2 cups sliced onion, separated into rings
1 cup chicken broth
¼ teaspoon salt
¼ teaspoon freshly ground pepper
2½ cups low-fat buttermilk
½ cup 50%-less-fat sour cream (such as Daisy Light)
½ cup chopped cucumber
¼ cup chopped green onions

1. Trim stems and roots from beets. Place beets in a large saucepan; add water to cover. Bring to a boil; cover, reduce heat, and simmer 1 hour or until beets are tender. Drain beets, and let cool slightly. Peel beets, and cut into ½-inch-thick slices; set aside.

2. Coat a large nonstick skillet with cooking spray; add margarine. Place over medium-high heat until margarine melts. Add onion; sauté 10 minutes or until tender.

3. Place half each of sliced beets, sautéed onion, chicken broth, salt, and pepper in a blender; process until mixture is smooth. Pour puréed beet mixture into a large bowl. Repeat procedure with remaining beets, sautéed onion, broth, salt, and pepper. Stir buttermilk into puréed beet mixture. Cover and chill at least 3 hours.

Chicken Salad in Cantaloupe

4. Ladle chilled soup into bowls. Top with sour cream, cucumber, and green onions. Yield: 8 servings (serving size: 1 cup soup, 1 tablespoon sour cream, 1 tablespoon cucumber, and 1½ teaspoons green onions).

Note: When you're short on time, you may substitute 3 (15-ounce) cans sliced beets, drained, if desired.

POINTS: 2; **Diabetic Exchanges:** 1 Starch, ½ Sk Milk
Per serving: CAL 125 (24% from fat); PRO 5.9g; FAT 3.3g (sat 0g); CARB 18.7g; FIB 1.6g; CHOL 5mg; IRON 1mg; SOD 341mg; CALC 141mg

Chicken Noodle Soup

Enjoy this soup all week long—the flavors get better with time.

1 tablespoon butter or stick margarine
1 cup peeled sliced carrot
1 cup peeled sliced parsnip
½ cup thinly sliced celery
1 tablespoon all-purpose flour
3½ cups chicken broth
1 cup water
¼ teaspoon salt
¼ teaspoon pepper
2 cups uncooked wide egg noodles
1 pound skinned, boned chicken breasts, cut into 1-inch pieces
2 tablespoons chopped fresh parsley

1. Melt butter in a large Dutch oven over medium-high heat. Add carrot, parsnip, and celery; sauté 3 minutes. Stir in flour. Gradually add broth, water, salt, and pepper, stirring with a whisk until well blended. Bring to a boil. Cover, reduce heat, and simmer 5 minutes. Add noodles and chicken, and bring to a boil. Cover, reduce heat, and simmer 10 minutes. Remove from heat; stir in parsley. Serve immediately or store in an airtight container in refrigerator. Yield: 8 servings (serving size: 1 cup).

POINTS: 3; **Diabetic Exchanges:** 2 V-L Meat, 1 Starch, 1 Veg
Per serving: CAL 169 (19% from fat); PRO 17g; FAT 3.5g (sat 1.7g); CARB 17.1g; FIB 1.6g; CHOL 48mg; IRON 1.4mg; SOD 527mg; CALC 32mg

Chicken Pasta Salad

3½ cups cooked small seashell macaroni, cooked without salt or fat
3 cups small fresh broccoli florets
1¾ cups trimmed fresh snow peas (about 6 ounces)
1⅔ cups chopped cooked chicken
1 cup red bell pepper strips
¼ cup sliced green onions
5 tablespoons red wine vinegar
3 tablespoons vegetable oil
2 tablespoons honey
2 teaspoons sesame seeds, toasted
1 teaspoon hot sauce
½ teaspoon salt
½ teaspoon ground ginger
3 garlic cloves, minced

1. Combine first 6 ingredients in a large bowl; toss well. Combine vinegar and next 7 ingredients in a small bowl; stir well. Pour dressing over pasta mixture; toss gently. Cover and chill at least 2 hours. Yield: 5 servings (serving size: 2 cups).

POINTS: 8; **Diabetic Exchanges:** 3 Starch, 2 L Meat, ½ Fat
Per serving: CAL 381 (27% from fat); PRO 22.3g; FAT 11.5g (sat 2.1g); CARB 46.4g; FIB 2.6g; CHOL 39mg; IRON 5.4mg; SOD 289mg; CALC 85mg

Only one pot is needed to make this quick-and-easy Chicken Noodle Soup.

Turkey-in-the-Slaw Sandwiches

The colorful slaw, generously spooned over mounds of turkey and encased in crisp toast, will ensure that you'll make these sandwiches again and again.

1   cup thinly sliced green cabbage
1   cup thinly sliced red cabbage
½   cup peeled shredded carrot
¼   cup light mayonnaise
¼   cup plain fat-free yogurt
1½ teaspoons sugar
¼   teaspoon white pepper
8   (1-ounce) slices whole wheat bread, toasted
2   tablespoons fat-free Thousand Island dressing
¾   pound thinly sliced cooked turkey breast

1. Combine first 7 ingredients in a bowl; stir well. Cover and chill.

2. Spread 1 side of 4 bread slices with dressing; top evenly with turkey and slaw. Top with remaining bread slices. Serve sandwiches immediately or store in small zip-top plastic bags in refrigerator until ready to serve. Yield: 4 servings.

POINTS: 6; **Diabetic Exchanges:** 2 Starch, 2 L Meat, 1 Veg
Per serving: CAL 298 (23% from fat); PRO 23.1g; FAT 7.5g (sat 1.3g); CARB 33.6g; FIB 3.2g; CHOL 7mg; IRON 3.5mg; SOD 1160mg; CALC 102mg

Couscous-and-Black Bean Salad

1   cup water
⅛   teaspoon salt
⅔   cup uncooked couscous
1   cup drained canned black beans
½   cup chopped red bell pepper
¼   cup chopped green onions
2   tablespoons chopped fresh parsley
¼   teaspoon grated orange rind
¼   cup orange juice

Turkey-in-the-Slaw
Sandwiches are an easy
way to incorporate
veggies into your lunch.

Crunchy Snack Mix

tablespoon seasoned rice vinegar
1½ teaspoons vegetable oil
¼ teaspoon ground cumin

1. Bring water and salt to a boil in a small saucepan; gradually stir in couscous. Remove from heat; cover and let stand 5 minutes. Fluff with a fork. Let cool slightly.

2. Combine couscous, beans, and next 4 ingredients in a bowl; toss well. Combine orange juice, vinegar, oil, and cumin; stir well. Pour dressing over couscous mixture; toss well. Cover and chill. Yield: 2 servings (serving size: 2 cups).

POINTS: 6; *Diabetic Exchanges:* 4 Starch, ½ V-L Meat
Per serving: CAL 342 (13% from fat); PRO 14.7g; FAT 4.8g (sat .8g); CARB 62.5g; FIB 6.6g; CHOL 0mg; IRON 3.9mg; SOD 391mg; CALC 46mg

Zesty Double-Bean Salad

1 (15.8-ounce) can Great Northern beans, rinsed and drained
1 (15-ounce) can black beans, rinsed and drained
1½ cups chopped plum tomato
1 cup chopped green bell pepper
1 cup sliced green onions
½ cup salsa
¼ cup red wine vinegar
2 tablespoons chopped fresh cilantro
½ teaspoon salt
½ teaspoon pepper

1. Combine all ingredients in a bowl; toss well. Serve at room temperature or chilled. Toss gently before serving. Yield: 6 servings (serving size: 1 cup).

POINTS: 1; *Diabetic Exchanges:* 1 Starch, ½ L Meat
Per serving: CAL 118 (7% from fat); PRO 6.6g; FAT 0.9g (sat 0g); CARB 14.7g; FIB 7.3g; CHOL 0mg; IRON 2.5mg; SOD 664mg; CALC 52mg

Crunchy Snack Mix

This crunchy snack is a great alternative to chips.

2 cups criss-cross of corn and rice cereal (such as Crispix)
2 cups crispy wheat cereal squares (such as Wheat Chex)
1½ cups tiny salted pretzels
½ cup unsalted, dry-roasted peanuts
2 tablespoons reduced-calorie stick margarine, melted

2 teaspoons Worcestershire sauce
½ teaspoon salt-free, extra spicy herb-and-spice blend
1 cup raisins

1. Preheat oven to 250°.

2. Combine first 4 ingredients in a large roasting pan. Combine margarine and Worcestershire sauce; pour over cereal mixture, tossing gently. Sprinkle with herb-and-spice blend; toss well. Bake at 250° for 30 minutes, stirring every 10 minutes. Remove from oven; stir in raisins. Let cool. Store in an airtight container. Yield: 14 servings (serving size: ½ cup).

POINTS: 3; *Diabetic Exchanges:* 1½ Starch, ½ Fat
Per serving: CAL 151 (30% from fat); PRO 3.5g; FAT 5g (sat 0.6g); CARB 25g; FIB 1.7g; CHOL 0mg; IRON 2.3mg; SOD 226mg; CALC 25mg

Blue Cheese, Turkey, and Rice Salad

3 cups water
1 (6-ounce) package wild rice
3 cups chopped fresh spinach
1¾ cups chopped cooked turkey breast
¾ cup (3 ounces) crumbled blue cheese
½ cup thinly sliced celery
½ cup drained chopped bottled roasted red bell peppers
2 tablespoons chopped pecans, toasted
¼ cup white wine vinegar
3 tablespoons chicken broth
2 tablespoons honey
1 tablespoon Dijon mustard
2 teaspoons hot sauce
1 teaspoon vegetable oil

1. Combine water and rice in a medium saucepan; bring to a boil. Cover, reduce heat, and simmer 50 minutes or until rice is tender. Drain well; let cool.

2. Combine rice, spinach, and next 5 ingredients in a large bowl; toss well. Combine vinegar and next 5 ingredients in a small bowl; stir well. Pour vinegar mixture over salad; toss well. Cover and chill. Yield: 4 servings (serving size: 1½ cups).

POINTS: 8; *Diabetic Exchanges:* 3 Starch, 3 L Meat
Per serving: CAL 415 (28% from fat); PRO 31.8g; FAT 12.7g (sat 5.1g); CARB 44.9g; FIB 4.5g; CHOL 59mg; IRON 3.2mg; SOD 775mg; CALC 190mg

Ham-and-Apple Sandwiches offer a slightly sweet change from typical lunch fare.

Ham-and-Apple Sandwiches

½   cup apple butter
2   teaspoons grated fresh onion
½   teaspoon dry mustard
8   (1-ounce) slices cinnamon-raisin bread, toasted
4   ounces thinly sliced lean ham
2   ounces Edam cheese, thinly sliced
1   small Red Delicious apple, cored and sliced crosswise into rings
Small apple wedges (optional)

1. Combine apple butter, onion, and mustard in a small bowl; stir well. Spread apple butter mixture evenly over 1 side of bread slices.

2. Divide ham, cheese, and apple rings evenly over 4 bread slices; top with remaining bread slices. Garnish with apple wedges, if desired. Yield: 4 servings.

POINTS: 6; **Diabetic Exchanges:** 3 Starch, 1 Fat, ½ Sk Milk
Per serving: CAL 324 (23% from fat); PRO 11.2g; FAT 8.3g (sat 3.6g); CARB 53.7g; FIB 3.4g; CHOL 23mg; IRON 1.8mg; SOD 697mg; CALC 146mg

Cucumber Vichyssoise

1   teaspoon reduced-calorie stick margarine
Cooking spray
3   cups sliced leek
2   cups sliced onion, separated into rings
2⅓ cups peeled, seeded, and coarsely chopped cucumber
1   cup water
2   cups peeled cubed baking potato
2   cups chicken broth

½   teaspoon salt
½   teaspoon white pepper
1   cup 1% low-fat milk
Thinly sliced cucumber (optional)
Chopped fresh chives (optional)

1. Melt margarine over medium-high heat in a large Dutch oven coated with cooking spray. Add leek and onion; sauté 15 minutes or until golden. Remove from pan; set aside.

2. Add chopped cucumber and 1 cup water to pan; bring to a boil. Cover, reduce heat, and simmer 10 minutes. Return leek mixture to pan. Add cubed potato and next 3 ingredients; bring to a boil. Cover, reduce heat, and simmer 10 minutes or until potato is tender. Remove from heat; let cool 10 minutes.

3. Pour one-third of cucumber mixture into a blender; process until smooth. Pour puréed cucumber mixture into a large bowl. Repeat procedure with remaining cucumber mixture. Stir milk into puréed cucumber mixture. Cover and chill.

4. Ladle chilled soup into bowls. Garnish with cucumber slices and chives, if desired. Yield: 8 servings (serving size: 1 cup).

POINTS: 2; **Diabetic Exchanges:** 1 Starch
Per serving: CAL 90 (14% from fat); PRO 3.3g; FAT 1.4g (sat 0.4g); CARB 16.6g; FIB 1.7g; CHOL 1mg; IRON 1.1mg; SOD 462mg; CALC 71mg

Focaccia Garden Sandwich

1   ounce sun-dried tomatoes, packed without oil (about 9)
½   cup hot water
1   (8-ounce) tub light jalapeño- or roasted garlic-flavored cream cheese, softened
3   tablespoons dill pickle relish
2   (10-ounce) packages thin Italian cheese-flavored pizza crusts (such as Boboli)
2¼ cups thinly sliced cucumber
1   cup peeled shredded carrot
1   cup alfalfa sprouts

1. Combine tomatoes and hot water in a small bowl; let stand 10 minutes. Drain and chop tomatoes. Combine tomatoes, cream cheese, and pickle relish in a bowl; stir well.

2. Spread cream cheese mixture evenly over 1 side of each crust. Arrange half of cucumber slices over 1 crust. Top with carrot, sprouts, remaining half of cucumber slices, and remaining crust, cream cheese side down. Wrap in plastic wrap, and chill. Cut into wedges. Yield: 6 servings.

POINTS: 8; Diabetic Exchanges: 2½ Starch, 2 Veg, 2 Fat, ½ Milk
Per serving: CAL 382 (28% from fat); PRO 16.9g; FAT 11.7g (sat 5.5g); CARB 51.3g; FIB 3.8g; CHOL 30mg; IRON 3.1mg; SOD 588mg; CALC 175mg

Tuna-and-Bow Tie Pasta Salad

4   cups cooked farfalle (about 8 ounces uncooked bow tie pasta), cooked without salt or fat
1   cup finely chopped tomato
½   cup peeled shredded carrot
½   cup finely chopped cucumber
¼   cup finely chopped celery
1   (9-ounce) can solid white tuna in water, drained and flaked
⅓   cup red wine vinegar
3   tablespoons water
1½ tablespoons Dijon mustard
1   tablespoon olive oil
¼   teaspoon pepper
⅛   teaspoon salt

1. Combine first 6 ingredients in a large bowl; toss well. Combine vinegar and next 5 ingredients; stir well. Pour vinegar mixture over pasta mixture; toss well. Cover and chill at least 2 hours. Toss gently before serving. Yield: 7 servings (serving size: 1 cup).

POINTS: 4; Diabetic Exchanges: 1 L Meat, 1½ Starch, 1 Veg
Per serving: CAL 195 (14% from fat); PRO 13.6g; FAT 3g (sat 0.4g); CARB 27.2g; FIB 1.5g; CHOL 20mg; IRON 2mg; SOD 432mg; CALC 18mg

Caesar Chicken-Salad Sandwiches

1   tablespoon fresh lemon juice, divided
2   teaspoons low-salt soy sauce
2   (4-ounce) skinned, boned chicken breast halves
Cooking spray
2   tablespoons grated Parmesan cheese
3   tablespoons light mayonnaise
1   teaspoon Dijon mustard
½   teaspoon anchovy paste
½   teaspoon bottled minced garlic
⅛   teaspoon pepper
4   (1.2-ounce) slices whole-grain bread
2   romaine lettuce leaves
4   (¼-inch-thick) slices tomato

1. Combine 2 teaspoons lemon juice and soy sauce in a shallow dish or pie plate. Add chicken, turning to coat. Cover and marinate in refrigerator 10 minutes, turning chicken over after 5 minutes. Remove chicken from dish; discard marinade.

2. Place chicken on a broiler pan coated with cooking spray; broil 6 minutes on each side or until done. Let cool; shred chicken with 2 forks.

3. Combine chicken, remaining 1 teaspoon lemon juice, cheese, and next 5 ingredients in a bowl; stir well. Spread 1 cup chicken mixture over each of 2 bread slices. Top each with 1 lettuce leaf, 2 tomato slices, and 1 bread slice. Serve immediately or store sandwiches in small zip-top plastic bags in refrigerator. Yield: 2 servings.

POINTS: 8; Diabetic Exchanges: 3 L Meat, 2½ Starch
Per serving: CAL 366 (28% from fat); PRO 30g; FAT 11.4g (sat 3.1g); CARB 37.3g; FIB 3g; CHOL 63mg; IRON 2.4mg; SOD 1,054mg; CALC 155mg

Imagine your coworkers' envy when you reach into your bag and pull out a Caesar Chicken-Salad Sandwich.

Spinach-Artichoke Pasta

1   (14-ounce) can artichoke hearts, drained
    and divided
1   tablespoon olive oil
1   tablespoon water
1   tablespoon lemon juice
½   teaspoon dried basil
¼   teaspoon dried oregano
¼   teaspoon pepper
1   garlic clove, minced
3   cups cooked radiatore (about 6 ounces
    uncooked, short, fat rippled pasta), cooked
    without salt or fat
2   cups thinly sliced fresh spinach
1   cup seeded chopped tomato
¼   cup (1 ounce) crumbled feta cheese

1. Combine 2 artichoke hearts, olive oil, and next 6 ingredients in a blender or food processor; process until smooth.

2. Chop remaining artichoke hearts. Combine chopped artichokes, pasta, spinach, and chopped tomato in a large bowl. Pour puréed artichoke mixture over pasta mixture; toss well to coat. Cover and chill at least 2 hours. Sprinkle with feta cheese before serving. Yield: 6 servings (serving size: 1 cup).

POINTS: 3; **Diabetic Exchanges:** 1½ Starch, 1 Veg, ½ Fat
Per serving: CAL 153 (23% from fat); PRO 5.9g; FAT 3.9g (sat 1.1g); CARB 24.9g; FIB 1.8g; CHOL 4mg; IRON 2.2mg; SOD 137mg; CALC 70mg

Ham-and-Rice Salad With Spinach

2   cups water
½   cup sweetened dried cranberries (such as
    Craisins)
1   (6.2-ounce) package fast-cooking recipe
    long-grain and wild rice (such as Uncle Ben's)
8   cups chopped fresh spinach
2   cups diced lean ham
½   cup chopped red onion
4   teaspoons olive oil
2   (11-ounce) cans mandarin oranges in light
    syrup, undrained

1. Combine first 3 ingredients in a medium saucepan, reserving seasoning packet from rice for another use. Bring to a boil; cover, reduce heat, and simmer 5 minutes or until liquid is absorbed. Let cool.

2. Combine rice mixture, spinach, and remaining ingredients in a bowl; toss well. Cover and chill. Yield: 4 servings (serving size: 2 cups).

Note: Stir the seasoning packet from the wild rice into plain white rice at another meal to give it an extra zip.

POINTS: 8; **Diabetic Exchanges:** 3 Starch, 1 Fat, 1 H-F Meat, ½ Sk Milk
Per serving: CAL 422 (20% from fat); PRO 17.4g; FAT 9.5g (sat 2g); CARB 72.3g; FIB 8.2g; CHOL 25mg; IRON 5.2mg; SOD 1,694mg; CALC 172mg

Jamaican Shrimp-and-Rice Salad

⅓   cup fresh lime juice
3   tablespoons low-salt Worcestershire sauce
1   tablespoon ketchup
2   teaspoons hot sauce
2   teaspoons vegetable oil
2   teaspoons molasses
¼   teaspoon freshly ground pepper
1   large garlic clove, crushed
3   cups cooked long-grain rice, cooked
    without salt or fat
¾   cup drained chopped bottled roasted red
    bell peppers (about 7 ounces)
½   cup chopped fresh cilantro
½   cup chopped green onions
1   (15-ounce) can black beans, rinsed and
    drained
1½ pounds medium shrimp, peeled
Cooking spray

1. Combine first 8 ingredients in a large bowl, and stir well. Reserve 1 tablespoon juice mixture to baste shrimp. Add rice, bell peppers, cilantro, green onions, and beans to remaining juice mixture in bowl; toss well. Set aside.

2. Place shrimp on a broiler pan coated with cooking spray; brush with reserved 1 tablespoon juice mixture. Broil 2 minutes on each side or until shrimp turn pink. Add shrimp to rice mixture; toss well. Serve immediately or store in an airtight container in refrigerator. Yield: 4 servings (serving size: 2 cups).

POINTS: 8; **Diabetic Exchanges:** 4 Starch, 3 V-L Meat
Per serving: CAL 426 (9% from fat); PRO 33.6g; FAT 4.4g (sat 1g); CARB 62.6g; FIB 4.6g; CHOL 207mg; IRON 7.2mg; SOD 1,306mg; CALC 126mg

Spinach-Artichoke Pasta

Marinated Vegetable Salad with roasted chicken.

Freezer Slaw

cups thinly sliced green cabbage
cup chopped green bell pepper
cup peeled shredded carrot
cup white wine vinegar
cup sugar
cup water
teaspoon celery seeds
teaspoon salt
teaspoon dry mustard

Combine first 3 ingredients in a bowl. Combine vinegar and next 5 ingredients in a saucepan; bring to a boil, and cook 1 minute. Pour hot vinegar mixture over cabbage mixture; toss well. Cover and chill. Serve chilled or spoon into small zip-top plastic bags, and freeze up to 1 month. Thaw in refrigerator, and serve with a slotted spoon. Yield: 8 servings (serving size: ½ cup).

POINTS: 1; Diabetic Exchanges: 1 Starch
Per serving: CAL 78 (3% from fat); PRO 1.1g; FAT 0.3g (sat 0g); CARB 18g; FIB 1.8g; CHOL 0mg; IRON 0.7mg; SOD 166mg; CALC mg

Curried Tofu-Egg Salad Sandwiches

Be sure to use the hot pepper sauce that contains whole peppers packed in vinegar.

cup finely chopped firm light tofu (about 5 ounces)
tablespoons chopped fresh cilantro
tablespoon chopped green onions
tablespoons light mayonnaise
tablespoons plain fat-free yogurt
teaspoon hot pepper sauce
teaspoon curry powder
teaspoon salt
teaspoon pepper
hard-cooked large eggs, finely chopped
(1.2-ounce) slices whole-grain bread

Combine first 10 ingredients in a bowl; stir well. Spread ½ cup tofu mixture evenly over each of 3 bread slices; top with remaining bread slices. Serve immediately or store in small zip-top plastic bags in refrigerator. Yield: 3 servings.

POINTS: 6; Diabetic Exchanges: 2 Starch, 1 V-L Meat, 1 Veg, 1 Fat
Per serving: CAL 272 (29% from fat); PRO 15g; FAT 8.9g (sat 2g); CARB 35.3g; FIB 3.3g; CHOL 147mg; IRON 2.6mg; SOD 29mg; CALC 127mg

Marinated Vegetable Salad

2   cups small fresh cauliflower florets
¾   cup peeled diagonally sliced carrot
1   cup diagonally sliced celery
½   cup red bell pepper strips
¼   cup sliced ripe olives
1   (14-ounce) can quartered artichoke hearts, drained
6   tablespoons white wine vinegar
1   teaspoon dried Italian seasoning
2   teaspoons olive oil
⅛   teaspoon crushed red pepper

1. Steam cauliflower and carrot, covered, 3 minutes or until crisp-tender. Rinse under cold water, and drain.

2. Combine steamed vegetables, celery, and next 3 ingredients in a bowl; toss gently. Combine vinegar and next 3 ingredients; stir well. Pour dressing over vegetables; toss gently. Cover and chill at least 4 hours. Yield: 6 servings (serving size: 1 cup).

POINTS: 1; Diabetic Exchanges: ½ Starch, ½ Fat
Per serving: CAL 60 (36% from fat); PRO 2g; FAT 2.4g (sat 0.4g); CARB 9g; FIB 2.3g; CHOL 0mg; IRON 1.5mg; SOD 202mg; CALC 50mg

Hearty Lentil Soup

A splash of balsamic vinegar enhances this soup packed with brown rice, lentils, and vegetables. Serve a bowlful with crackers for a quick and satisfying lunch.

8   cups beef broth
1   (28-ounce) can tomatoes, undrained and chopped
2   cups peeled diced carrot
1½   cups dried lentils
1   cup uncooked brown rice
1   cup chopped onion
½   cup chopped celery
½   teaspoon dried basil
½   teaspoon dried oregano
¼   teaspoon dried thyme
3   garlic cloves, minced
2   bay leaves
½   cup chopped fresh parsley
2   tablespoons balsamic vinegar
1   teaspoon salt
½   teaspoon pepper
¼   cup grated Parmesan cheese

1. Bring broth to a boil in a large Dutch oven. Add tomatoes and next 10 ingredients; stir well. Return to a boil; cover, reduce heat, and simmer 45 minutes or until rice is tender. Remove from heat; stir in parsley and next 3 ingredients. Discard bay leaves.

2. Ladle soup into bowls; sprinkle with cheese. Yield: 12 servings (serving size: 1 cup soup and 1 teaspoon cheese).

POINTS: 3; **Diabetic Exchanges:** 2 Veg, 1½ Starch, 1 V-L Meat
Per serving: CAL 198 (6% from fat); PRO 13.4g; FAT 1.4g (sat 0.5g); CARB 34.1g; FIB 4.7g; CHOL 1mg; IRON 3.6mg; SOD 753mg; CALC 86mg

French-Style Beef and Pasta

3   cups cooked farfalle (about 6 ounces uncooked bow tie pasta), cooked without salt or fat
2   cups diced zucchini
2   cups chopped plum tomato
⅓   cup chopped fresh parsley
4   ounces sliced lean deli roast beef, cut into ½-inch-wide strips
¼   cup red wine vinegar
3   tablespoons beef broth
1½ tablespoons extra-virgin olive oil
1   tablespoon honey mustard
½   teaspoon pepper
¼   teaspoon salt

1. Combine pasta, zucchini, tomato, parsley, and beef in a bowl; toss well. Combine vinegar and next 5 ingredients; stir well. Pour over pasta mixture; toss well. Serve at room temperature or chilled. Yield: 4 servings (serving size: 2 cups).

POINTS: 5; **Diabetic Exchanges:** 2 Starch, 1 Veg, 1 Fat, ½ L Meat
Per serving: CAL 268 (30% from fat); PRO 12.3g; FAT 8.9g (sat 1.6g); CARB 35.9g; FIB 3.6g; CHOL 23mg; IRON 3.4mg; SOD 466mg; CALC 34mg

Smoked-Salmon Sandwiches

2   ounces smoked salmon
⅓   cup light cream cheese
1   teaspoon lemon juice
2   teaspoons chopped fresh or ½ teaspoon dried dill
2   teaspoons minced red onion
4   (1-ounce) slices pumpernickel bread
4   (⅛-inch-thick) slices tomato
8   (⅛-inch-thick) slices cucumber

1. Combine first 3 ingredients in a food processor; process until smooth. Spoon into a bowl; st in dill and onion.

2. Spread salmon mixture evenly over 2 brea slices; top each with 2 tomato slices, 4 cucumb slices, and 1 bread slice. Serve immediately store in small zip-top plastic bags in refrigerat until ready to serve. Yield: 2 servings.

POINTS: 5; **Diabetic Exchanges:** 2 Starch, 1 Veg, 1 L Meat, ½ Fat
Per serving: CAL 265 (28% from fat); PRO 14.7g; FAT 8.3g (s 4.1g); CARB 35g; FIB 4g; CHOL 29mg; IRON 2mg; SOD 760m CALC 112mg

Mediterranean Lentil Salad
You'll find plenty of fiber in this salad.

4   cups water
1   cup dried lentils
1¾ cups drained, coarsely chopped bottled roasted red bell peppers
¼   cup sliced green onions
¼   cup balsamic vinegar
¼   cup chicken broth
1   tablespoon olive oil
1   teaspoon dried basil
¼   teaspoon salt
¼   teaspoon pepper
1   garlic clove, minced
8   romaine lettuce leaves
¼   cup (1 ounce) crumbled goat cheese

1. Combine 4 cups water and lentils in saucepan; bring to a boil. Cover, reduce heat, an simmer 30 minutes or until tender. Drain; rins under cold water, and set aside.

2. Combine lentils, bell peppers, and next 8 in gredients in a bowl; toss gently. Cover and chill least 2 hours. Serve on lettuce-lined plates; sprin kle with goat cheese. Yield: 4 servings (servin size: 2 lettuce leaves, 1 cup lentil mixture, and tablespoon cheese).

POINTS: 4; **Diabetic Exchanges:** 2 Starch, 1 Veg, 1 V-L Meat, 1 Fat
Per serving: CAL 250 (23% from fat); PRO 16g; FAT 6.5g (sa 2g); CARB 34.9g; FIB 6.7g; CHOL 6mg; IRON 5.7mg; SOD 259m CALC 63mg

Mediterranean Lentil Salad with flatbread crackers

Greek Spaghetti With Tomatoes and Feta

Hummus

½ cup 1% low-fat cottage cheese
¼ cup fresh parsley leaves
2 tablespoons tahini (sesame-seed paste)
¼ teaspoon grated lemon rind
1 tablespoon fresh lemon juice
½ teaspoon ground coriander
⅛ teaspoon salt
1 garlic clove
1 (15-ounce) can chickpeas (garbanzo beans), drained

1. Place all ingredients in a food processor; process until smooth. Store in an airtight container in refrigerator. Serve with pita bread or fresh vegetables. Yield: 4 servings (serving size: ½ cup).

POINTS: 4; **Diabetic Exchanges:** 1½ Starch, 1 V-L Meat, ½ Fat
Per serving: CAL 184 (30% from fat); PRO 11.2g; FAT 6.1g (sat 0.9g); CARB 22.7g; FIB 3.4g; CHOL 1mg; IRON 3mg; SOD 342mg; CALC 92mg

Sesame Beef-Quinoa Salad

1 cup uncooked quinoa
Cooking spray
2 cups water
2 tablespoons sesame seeds
1 teaspoon curry powder
½ cup orange juice
3 tablespoons lime juice
1 tablespoon peeled grated fresh ginger
1 tablespoon beef broth or water
1 teaspoon dark sesame oil
½ teaspoon salt
¼ teaspoon pepper
2 cups (½-inch) cubed lean deli roast beef (about 12 ounces)
1½ cups peeled finely chopped carrot
1½ cups finely chopped green cabbage
½ cup minced green onions
8 curly leaf lettuce leaves (optional)

1. Place quinoa in a fine sieve; rinse under cold water. Drain well; set aside.

2. Place quinoa in a large nonstick skillet coated with cooking spray; sauté over medium heat until lightly browned.

3. Bring 2 cups water to a boil in a medium saucepan. Add quinoa; cover, reduce heat, and simmer 12 minutes or until liquid is absorbed and quinoa is tender. Spoon into a large bowl; set aside.

4. Place sesame seeds in skillet coated with cooking spray; cook over medium heat until lightly browned, stirring constantly. Add to quinoa.

5. Place curry powder in skillet; cook over medium heat 2 minutes or until fragrant, stirring constantly. Stir in orange juice, lime juice, and ginger; bring to a boil. Remove from heat; stir in broth and next 3 ingredients. Add juice mixture, beef, and next 3 ingredients to quinoa mixture; toss well. Cover and chill. Stir before serving. Serve on lettuce-lined plates, if desired. Yield: 4 servings (serving size: 2 cups).

POINTS: 7; **Diabetic Exchanges:** 3 L Meat, 2½ Starch, 1 Veg
Per serving: CAL 389 (26% from fat); PRO 30g; FAT 11.2g (sat 2.6g); CARB 43.3g; FIB 9.1g; CHOL 51mg; IRON 7.3mg; SOD 394mg; CALC 119mg

Greek Spaghetti With Tomatoes and Feta

2 teaspoons olive oil
1 teaspoon dried oregano
1 large garlic clove, minced
3 cups diced tomato
½ cup sliced green onions
¼ cup chopped fresh parsley, divided
2 tablespoons lemon juice
4 cups cooked thin spaghetti (about 8 ounces uncooked), cooked without salt or fat
1 cup (4 ounces) crumbled feta cheese, divided
Freshly ground pepper (optional)

1. Heat oil in a large nonstick skillet over medium-high heat. Add oregano and garlic, and sauté 30 seconds. Add tomato, green onions, 2 tablespoons parsley, and lemon juice; cook 2 minutes or until heated.

2. Combine tomato mixture, spaghetti, and ¾ cup cheese; toss gently. Top with remaining ¼ cup cheese and 2 tablespoons parsley, and sprinkle with pepper, if desired. Serve at room temperature or store in an airtight container in refrigerator. Yield: 4 servings (serving size: 1¼ cups).

POINTS: 7; **Diabetic Exchanges:** 3 Starch, 1½ Fat, 1 Veg
Per serving: CAL 334 (26% from fat); PRO 12.5g; FAT 9.8g (sat 4.8g); CARB 50.2g; FIB 4.8g; CHOL 25mg; IRON 3.4mg; SOD 336mg; CALC 179mg

Break the Cycle

A WAVE OF CREATIVE DISHES STEERS
DINNER IN A NEW DIRECTION.

"*What's for dinner?" You may find yourself cycling the same five or six meals around the table every week just to have a quick answer to that question. But trying a new recipe when you're tired at the end of the day may seem overwhelming.*

We anticipated this dilemma and have compiled 35 fresh dinner ideas to turn the "same-old same-old" meal routine inside out. Tasty, but minor, variations on familiar dishes, such as lasagna, burgers, and French fries, will ensure a thumbs up from skeptical kids. Creamy Ham-and-Chicken Lasagna, Tuna Burgers, and Oven Fries are just a few of your options. So the next time you hear your family ask "the question," you'll be able to surprise them.

Pair Three-Bean Enchiladas with a simple salad of lettuce, tomato, avocado, and ripe olives for a hearty, meatless meal.

Tossed Salad Supreme

Three-Bean Enchiladas

1½ cups drained canned kidney beans
1½ cups drained canned navy beans
1½ cups drained canned pinto beans
½ cup chopped onion
¼ cup canned vegetable broth or water
1 teaspoon chili powder
1 teaspoon ground cumin
¼ teaspoon salt
2 garlic cloves, peeled
1 (4-ounce) can chopped green chiles, undrained
2 (10-ounce) cans enchilada sauce
12 (6-inch) corn tortillas
Cooking spray
½ cup (2 ounces) shredded reduced-fat Monterey Jack cheese

1. Preheat oven to 350°.

2. Place first 10 ingredients in a food processor; process 5 seconds or until mixture is chunky.

3. Pour 1 can enchilada sauce in a medium skillet. Place over medium heat until warm. Working with 1 tortilla at a time, dip each tortilla in warm sauce. Spoon ⅓ cup bean mixture down center of each tortilla, and roll up. Place enchiladas, seam side down, in a 13- x 9-inch baking dish coated with cooking spray. Pour remaining warm enchilada sauce and remaining can of enchilada sauce over enchiladas; cover and bake at 350° for 20 minutes. Uncover; sprinkle with cheese, and bake an additional 5 minutes. Yield: 6 servings.

POINTS: 6; **Diabetic Exchanges:** 3 Starch, 1 Sk Milk, 1 Veg
Per serving: CAL 360 (11% from fat); PRO 18.7g; FAT 4.3g (sat 1.4g); CARB 65.2g; FIB 8.9g; CHOL 7mg; IRON 6mg; SOD 1,111mg; CALC 256mg

Tossed Salad Supreme

Make the salad and the dressing up to four hours before serving; chill them in separate containers.

12 cups torn mixed bitter salad greens (such as arugula, curly endive, radicchio, and watercress)
⅓ cup (1⅓ ounces) crumbled feta cheese
¼ cup chopped fresh basil
3 plum tomatoes, each quartered lengthwise
3 tablespoons chicken broth
2 tablespoons balsamic vinegar
1½ teaspoons olive oil

¼ teaspoon sugar
¼ teaspoon salt
¼ teaspoon freshly ground pepper
1 garlic clove, minced

1. Combine first 4 ingredients in a large bowl; toss gently.

2. Combine broth and next 6 ingredients; stir well. Pour over salad; toss gently. Yield: 6 servings (serving size: about 2 cups).

POINTS: 1; **Diabetic Exchanges:** 1 Veg, ½ Fat
Per serving: CAL 57 (46% from fat); PRO 3.2g; FAT 2.9g (sat 1.1g); CARB 5.7g; FIB 2.5g; CHOL 5mg; IRON 1.6mg; SOD 182mg; CALC 78mg

Grilled Jalapeño Chicken

⅓ cup fresh lime juice
¼ cup honey
2 tablespoons fresh cilantro leaves
2 tablespoons soy sauce
¼ teaspoon salt
¼ teaspoon pepper
3 jalapeño peppers, halved and seeded
3 garlic cloves, chopped
6 (6-ounce) skinned chicken breast halves (bone-in)
Cooking spray

1. Place first 8 ingredients in a blender; process until smooth. Combine lime juice mixture and chicken in a large, heavy-duty zip-top plastic bag. Seal bag, and marinate chicken in refrigerator 1 to 8 hours.

2. Prepare grill. Remove chicken from bag, reserving marinade. Place chicken on grill rack coated with cooking spray; cover and grill 12 minutes on each side or until done, basting occasionally with reserved marinade. Yield: 6 servings.

POINTS: 3; **Diabetic Exchanges:** 3 V-L Meat, 1 Starch
Per serving: CAL 159 (15% from fat); PRO 26.7g; FAT 2.6g (sat 1.1g); CARB 14.3g; FIB 0.1g; CHOL 62mg; IRON 1.2mg; SOD 345mg; CALC 20mg

Bean-and-Barley Soup

Smoked turkey sausage adds considerable flavor to this healthy, high-fiber soup.

1 tablespoon olive oil
1 cup chopped onion
1 cup chopped carrot

½   cup chopped celery
2   garlic cloves, minced
½   cup uncooked pearl barley
¼   pound smoked turkey sausage, cut into
    ½-inch cubes
2   cups frozen baby lima beans
1¾ cups water
⅛   teaspoon pepper
2   (14¼-ounce) cans fat-free chicken broth
1   (14.5-ounce) can diced tomatoes,
    undrained
½   teaspoon hot sauce

1. Heat oil in a large Dutch oven over medium-high heat. Add onion and next 3 ingredients; sauté 5 minutes. Add barley and sausage; sauté 4 minutes. Add beans and next 4 ingredients; bring to a boil. Reduce heat, and simmer, uncovered, 45 minutes. Remove from heat; stir in hot sauce. Yield: 6 servings (serving size: 1½ cups).

POINTS: 4; **Diabetic Exchanges:** 2 Starch, 1 V-L Meat, 1 Fat
Per serving: CAL 228 (26% from fat); PRO 13.4g; FAT 6.7g (sat 1.6g); CARB 29.5g; FIB 4.9g; CHOL 16mg; IRON 2.4mg; SOD 423mg; CALC 78mg

Cheesy Lentils and Rice

Add crusty bread and a salad to make a satisfying meatless meal.

3   cups water
1   cup dried lentils
1   teaspoon reduced-calorie stick margarine
1   cup chopped onion
1   cup chopped green bell pepper
2   garlic cloves, minced
1   (14.5-ounce) can diced tomatoes,
    undrained
½   cup water
1   teaspoon paprika
½   teaspoon black pepper
½   teaspoon ground red pepper
¼   teaspoon salt
2   cups hot cooked brown rice, cooked
    without salt or fat
Cooking spray
1½ cups (6 ounces) shredded cheddar cheese

1. Preheat oven to 325°.

2. Combine 3 cups water and lentils in a medium saucepan; bring to a boil. Partially cover, reduce heat, and simmer 15 minutes or until almost tender. Drain lentils; set aside.

3. Melt margarine in a large nonstick skillet over medium heat. Add onion, bell pepper, and garlic; sauté 7 minutes until tender. Add lentils, tomatoes, and next 5 ingredients; stir well. Cover, reduce heat, and simmer 5 minutes, stirring occasionally.

4. Spoon rice into a 2-quart baking dish coated with cooking spray; pour lentil mixture over rice. Cover and bake at 325° for 15 minutes. Sprinkle with cheddar cheese; cover and bake an additional 5 minutes. Yield: 7 servings (serving size: 1 cup).

POINTS: 6; **Diabetic Exchanges:** 2 Starch, ½ Sk Milk, 1½ V-L Meat, 1 Fat
Per serving: CAL 290 (29% from fat); PRO 16.3g; FAT 9.3g (sat 5.2g); CARB 36.5g; FIB 4.5g; CHOL 26mg; IRON 3.7mg; SOD 319mg; CALC 224mg

Fettuccine Alfredo

Serve this dish piping hot while it's creamiest.

1   tablespoon butter or stick margarine
2   small garlic cloves, minced
1   tablespoon all-purpose flour
1⅓ cups fat-free milk
2   tablespoons light cream cheese
1¼ cups (3 ounces) finely shredded fresh
    Parmesan cheese, divided
4   cups hot cooked fettuccine (about 8
    ounces uncooked pasta), cooked without
    salt or fat
2   teaspoons chopped fresh flat-leaf parsley
Freshly ground pepper

1. Melt butter in a saucepan over medium heat. Add garlic; sauté 1 minute. Stir in flour. Gradually add milk, stirring with a whisk until blended. Cook 8 minutes or until thick and bubbly, stirring constantly. Add cream cheese; cook 2 minutes, stirring constantly. Add 1 cup Parmesan cheese, stirring constantly until cheese melts. Pour over fettuccine; toss well to coat. Sprinkle with remaining ¼ cup Parmesan cheese, parsley, and pepper. Serve immediately. Yield: 4 servings (serving size: 1 cup).

POINTS: 7; **Diabetic Exchanges:** 3 Starch, 1 H-F Meat
Per serving: CAL 345 (25% from fat); PRO 16.8g; FAT 9.7g (sat 4.4g); CARB 46.7g; FIB 2.3g; CHOL 18mg; IRON 2.3mg; SOD 401mg; CALC 333mg

Fettuccine Alfredo

Greek Pork Tenderloin Salad

This light meal is perfect for summertime.

1   pound pork tenderloin
1½ tablespoons red wine vinegar
1   teaspoon chopped fresh oregano
1½ teaspoons olive oil
1   garlic clove, crushed
1   (8-ounce) carton plain fat-free yogurt
1½ cups peeled sliced cucumber, divided
1   tablespoon chopped fresh dill
Cooking spray
4   cups torn romaine lettuce
½   cup thinly sliced onion, separated into
       rings
½   cup thinly sliced radishes
2   medium tomatoes, each cut into
       8 wedges
1   medium green bell pepper, cut crosswise
       into 12 rings
8   ripe olives, pitted
2   tablespoons (½ ounce) crumbled feta
       cheese
2   teaspoons chopped fresh mint

A cool, cucumber-yogurt dressing tops this Greek Pork Tenderloin Salad.

1. Trim fat from pork. Combine vinegar, oregano, oil, and garlic in a shallow dish; stir well. Add pork, turning to coat. Cover and marinate in refrigerator 30 minutes, turning pork occasionally.

2. Place yogurt, ½ cup cucumber, and dill in food processor; process 10 seconds or unt[il] smooth. Set dressing aside.

3. Prepare grill. Remove pork from dish, reserv[ing] marinade. Place pork on grill rack coate[d] with cooking spray. Cover and grill 30 minutes o[r] until an instant-read meat thermometer register[s] 160° (pork will be slightly pink), turning por[k] occasionally and basting with reserved marinade. Thinly slice pork; set aside.

4. Place 1 cup lettuce on each of 4 plates; to[p] each salad with one-fourth of pork, ¼ cup cu[-] cumber, one-fourth of onion, 2 tablespoon[s] radishes, 4 tomato wedges, 3 bell pepper ring[s] and 2 olives. Sprinkle each salad with 1½ tea[-] spoons feta cheese and ½ teaspoon mint. Spoo[n] about 6 tablespoons dressing over each sala[d.] Serve immediately. Yield: 4 servings.

POINTS: 5; **Diabetic Exchanges:** 3½ V-L Meat, 3 Veg, 1 Fat
Per serving: CAL 252 (29% from fat); PRO 30.6g; FAT 8.2g (sa[t] 2.5g); CARB 14.3g; FIB 3g; CHOL 83mg; IRON 3.2mg; SO[D] 228mg; CALC 192mg

Triple-Corn Spoon Bread

This moist, slightly sweet dish is a cross between corn bread dressing and creamed corn.

1 cup fat-free sour cream
3 tablespoons butter or stick margarine, melted
1 large egg
½ cup chopped onion
1 (15.25-ounce) can no-salt-added whole-kernel corn, undrained
1 (14¾-ounce) can no-salt-added cream-style corn
1 (8½-ounce) package corn muffin mix
Cooking spray

1. Preheat oven to 350°.
2. Combine first 3 ingredients in a large bowl; stir well with a whisk. Stir in onion and next 3 ingredients. Pour into an 8-inch square baking dish coated with cooking spray. Bake at 350° for 1 hour or until spoon bread is set and lightly browned. Yield: 8 servings.

POINTS: 6; **Diabetic Exchanges:** 2½ Starch
Per serving: CAL 262 (30% from fat); PRO 6.2g; FAT 8.6g (sat 2.2g); CARB 39.3g; FIB 1.6g; CHOL 28mg; IRON 1.2mg; SOD 322mg; CALC 15mg

Sesame-Soy Marinated Flank Steak

1 (1½-pound) lean flank steak
¼ cup finely chopped green onions
¼ cup low-salt soy sauce
2 tablespoons sugar
2 tablespoons sherry
1 tablespoon dark sesame oil
1 tablespoon water
¼ teaspoon coarsely ground pepper
4 garlic cloves, crushed
Cooking spray

1. Trim fat from steak. Combine steak and next 8 ingredients in a large zip-top plastic bag. Seal bag, and marinate in refrigerator 8 hours, turning bag occasionally.
2. Prepare grill. Remove steak from bag, reserving marinade. Place steak on grill rack coated with cooking spray; grill 7 minutes on each side or until desired degree of doneness, basting frequently with reserved marinade. Cut steak diagonally across grain into thin slices. Yield: 6 servings (serving size: 3 ounces).

POINTS: 6; **Diabetic Exchanges:** 3 M-F Meat
Per serving: CAL 223 (55% from fat); PRO 21.9g; FAT 13.6g (sat 5.4g); CARB 2.1g; FIB 0.2g; CHOL 60mg; IRON 2.3mg; SOD 203mg; CALC 8mg

WORKING WITH GARLIC:

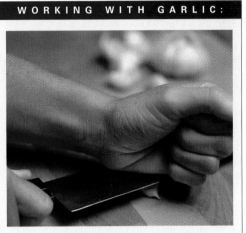

Mash garlic by crushing it under the weight of your hand on a chef's knife. The skin should slip right off.

Chop peeled garlic into very fine irregular pieces, using the knife's blade to pull pieces back into the pile until minced.

Pesto-Topped Orange Roughy

Try this flavorful herbed mixture on any mild-flavored fish like cod, catfish, snapper, or grouper.

⅔ cup dry breadcrumbs
2½ tablespoons prepared pesto (such as Pesto Sanremo)
¼ teaspoon pepper
4 (6-ounce) orange roughy fillets
Cooking spray

1. Preheat oven to 400°.

2. Place breadcrumbs in a shallow dish or pie plate. Combine pesto and pepper; brush over fish. Dredge fish in breadcrumbs, and place in an 11- x 7-inch baking dish coated with cooking spray. Coat fish with cooking spray. Bake at 400° for 15 minutes or until fish flakes easily when tested with a fork. Yield: 4 servings.

POINTS: 5; **Diabetic Exchanges:** 3½ V-L Meat, 1 Starch, 1 Fat
Per serving: CAL 238 (27% from fat); PRO 27.6g; FAT 7.1g (sat 7.1g); CARB 15g; FIB 0.9g; CHOL 34mg; IRON 2.6mg; SOD 366mg; CALC 114mg

Barbecued Shrimp

Rosemary adds a lemony-pine flavor to the savory-sweet marinade that coats these shrimp. We used very large shrimp, but you may substitute a smaller size—just adjust the cooking time accordingly.

Olive oil-flavored cooking spray
¼   cup diced onion
½   cup ketchup
2   tablespoons chopped fresh rosemary
1   tablespoon brown sugar
1   tablespoon dry mustard
1   tablespoon white vinegar
¼   teaspoon garlic powder
Dash of hot sauce
1½ pounds jumbo shrimp (about 24), peeled
Cooking spray

1. Coat a nonstick skillet with cooking spray; place over medium-high heat until hot. Add onion; sauté 3 minutes or until tender. Remove from heat; stir in ketchup and next 6 ingredients. Let stand 2 hours.

2. Place shrimp in a large shallow dish. Pour ketchup mixture over shrimp, stirring to coat. Cover and chill 1 hour. Thread tail and neck of each shrimp onto skewers so shrimp will lie flat.

3. Prepare grill. Place skewers on grill rack coated with cooking spray; grill 3 minutes on each side or until shrimp are done. Yield: 4 servings (serving size: 6 shrimp).

POINTS: 3; **Diabetic Exchanges:** 3 V-L Meat, ½ Starch
Per serving: CAL 156 (15% from fat); PRO 22.7g; FAT 2.6g (sat 0.6g); CARB 9.5g; FIB 0.8g; CHOL 166mg; IRON 5.7mg; SOD 384mg; CALC 72mg

Oven Fries

1½ pounds baking potatoes, cut into thin strips
1   tablespoon vegetable oil
1   teaspoon salt
Cooking spray

1. Preheat oven to 450°.

2. Pat potato strips dry with paper towels, and place in a large bowl. Drizzle oil over potatoes, and sprinkle with salt; toss well. Arrange potatoes in a single layer on a large baking sheet or jelly-roll pan coated with cooking spray. Bake at 450° for 15 minutes. Turn potatoes with a spatula, and bake an additional 15 minutes or until lightly browned, turning every 5 minutes. Yield: 4 servings.

POINTS: 3; **Diabetic Exchanges:** 2 Starch
Per serving: CAL 158 (21% from fat); PRO 3.7g; FAT 3.7g (sat 0.7g); CARB 28.2g; FIB 3.1g; CHOL 0mg; IRON 2.2mg; SOD 598mg; CALC 22mg

Chili Fries Variation: Combine 2 teaspoons chili powder, 1 teaspoon salt, ½ teaspoon dried oregano, ¼ teaspoon garlic powder, and ¼ teaspoon ground cumin in a small bowl; stir well. Sprinkle spice mixture over oiled potatoes; toss well. Yield: 4 servings. *POINTS:* 3

Cheese Fries Variation: Combine 2 tablespoons grated Parmesan cheese, ½ teaspoon salt, ¼ teaspoon garlic powder, ¼ teaspoon paprika, and ¼ teaspoon pepper in a small bowl; stir well. Sprinkle cheese mixture over oiled potatoes; toss well. Yield: 4 servings. *POINTS:* 3

Tuna Burgers

Here's a healthy and flavorful alternative to beef hamburgers.

1   (9-ounce) can tuna in water, drained and flaked
½   cup coarsely crushed saltine crackers (about 11 crackers)
¼   cup finely chopped green bell pepper
2   tablespoons finely chopped celery
2   tablespoons finely chopped onion
¼   teaspoon pepper
1   large egg, lightly beaten
Cooking spray
1   teaspoon vegetable oil

Barbecued Shrimp and Oven Fries with coleslaw

Oats and honey add texture and sweetness to Whole-Grain Pan Rolls.

2   tablespoons tartar sauce
4   (1½-ounce) hamburger buns, split and toasted
4   curly leaf lettuce leaves
8   (¼-inch-thick) slices tomato

1. Combine first 7 ingredients in a bowl; stir well. Divide mixture into 4 equal portions, shaping each portion into a patty.

2. Coat a large nonstick skillet with cooking spray; add oil, and place over medium-high heat until hot. Add patties; cook 2 minutes on each side or until browned.

3. Spread tartar sauce evenly over cut sides of buns. Place patties on bottom halves of buns; top with lettuce leaves, tomato slices, and top halves of buns. Yield: 4 servings.

POINTS: 6; **Diabetic Exchanges**: 2 Starch, 2 L Meat, ½ Fat
Per serving: CAL 295 (29% from fat); PRO 21.8g; FAT 9.6g (sat 1.4g); CARB 29.7g; FIB 1.9g; CHOL 76mg; IRON 2.9mg; SOD 482mg; CALC 77mg

Whole-Grain Pan Rolls

1   cup water
¼   cup honey
¼   cup butter or stick margarine
¾   cup whole wheat flour
½   cup regular oats
1   teaspoon salt
2   packages dry yeast
1   large egg
2¼ to 2½ cups all-purpose flour
Cooking spray

1. Combine first 3 ingredients in a small saucepan. Place over medium heat, and cook until butter melts. Remove from heat; let mixture cool to 120° to 130°.

2. Combine whole wheat flour, oats, salt, and yeast in a large bowl; stir well. Gradually add hot butter mixture; beat at low speed of a heavy-duty stand mixer 1 minute. Add egg; beat at medium speed of mixer 2 minutes. Gradually add enough ll-purpose flour to form a soft dough.

3. Turn dough out onto a floured surface; knead until smooth and elastic (about 8 minutes). Divide dough into 24 equal portions, shaping each portion into a ball; place in a 13- x 9-inch baking pan coated with cooking spray. Cover and let rise in a warm place (85°), free from drafts, 1 hour or until doubled in bulk.

4. Preheat oven to 375°.

5. Bake rolls at 375° for 20 minutes or until lightly browned. Yield: 2 dozen (serving size: 1 roll).

POINTS: 2; **Diabetic Exchanges:** 1 Starch
Per serving: CAL 99 (23% from fat); PRO 2.7g; FAT 2.5g (sat .3g); CARB 16.9g; FIB 1.2g; CHOL 14mg; IRON 1mg; SOD 21mg; CALC 6mg

Peppered Pork Chop Casserole

7   (4-ounce) lean center-cut loin pork chops
    (about ½ inch thick)
½   teaspoon salt
¼   teaspoon pepper
1   tablespoon vegetable oil
1½ cups uncooked long-grain rice
Cooking spray
1   cup chopped green bell pepper
1   cup water
½   cup chopped onion
½   teaspoon salt
¼   teaspoon pepper
1   garlic clove, minced
1   (15-ounce) can tomato sauce
1   (14½-ounce) can Italian-style stewed
    tomatoes, undrained and chopped
6   (¼-inch-thick) green bell pepper rings

1. Preheat oven to 350°.

2. Sprinkle chops with ½ teaspoon salt and ¼ teaspoon pepper. Heat oil in a large nonstick skillet over medium-high heat. Add chops; cook 4 minutes on each side or until browned. Remove chops from skillet; set aside.

3. Spread rice evenly in a 13- x 9-inch baking dish coated with cooking spray. Combine chopped bell pepper and next 7 ingredients, and stir well. Pour tomato mixture over rice. Arrange chops over tomato mixture; top each chop with a bell pepper ring. Cover and bake at 350° for 1 hour or

until chops and rice are tender. Yield: 7 servings (serving size: 1 chop and 1 cup rice mixture).

POINTS: 9; **Diabetic Exchanges:** 3 L Meat, 2½ Starch, 1 Fat
Per serving: CAL 406 (32% from fat); PRO 27.2g; FAT 14.3g (sat 4.5g); CARB 40.7g; FIB 2.2g; CHOL 77mg; IRON 3.7mg; SOD 840mg; CALC 51mg

Chuckwagon Beans

2   (15-ounce) cans pork and beans
2   cups finely chopped onion
1   cup finely chopped green bell pepper
¾   cup ketchup
½   cup firmly packed brown sugar
½   cup molasses
1   teaspoon barbeque smoked seasoning
    (such as Hickory Liquid Smoke)
Dash of hot sauce
Cooking spray

1. Preheat oven to 425°.

2. Combine all ingredients except cooking spray in a bowl; stir well. Spoon into a shallow 2-quart casserole coated with cooking spray. Bake, uncovered, at 425° for 40 minutes or until bubbly. Yield: 7 servings (servings size: about ¾ cup).

POINTS: 4; **Diabetic Exchanges:** 4 Starch
Per serving: CAL 272 (5% from fat); PRO 7.6g; FAT 1.6g (sat 0.6g); CARB 62g; FIB 8.4g; CHOL 9mg; IRON 5.9mg; SOD 889mg; CALC 146mg

Peppered Lamb Chops

8   (4-ounce) lean lamb loin chops
1   tablespoon cracked pepper
3   tablespoons finely chopped green onion
2   tablespoons coarse-grained mustard
1   tablespoon low-salt soy sauce
1   garlic clove, minced
Cooking spray

1. Trim fat from chops. Combine pepper and next 4 ingredients in a small bowl; stir well. Spread mixture over 1 side of each chop.

2. Prepare grill. Place chops, coated side up, on grill rack coated with cooking spray; grill 5 minutes on each side or until desired degree of doneness. Yield: 4 servings.

POINTS: 6; **Diabetic Exchanges:** 4½ L Meat
Per serving: CAL 258 (40% from fat); PRO 33.7g; FAT 11.5g (sat 3.9g); CARB 2.4g; FIB 0.5g; CHOL 105mg; IRON 3.2mg; SOD 467mg; CALC 33mg

Peking Pork Tenderloin

The pork takes on a pronounced ginger flavor as it marinates. Two tenderloins, about the size you'll need for this recipe, typically come packaged together at the meat counter.

2   (¾-pound) pork tenderloins
¼   cup soy sauce
1½ teaspoons peeled grated fresh ginger
2   garlic cloves, crushed
⅓   cup honey
⅓   cup sesame seeds, toasted (about a
      2.4-ounce jar)
Cooking spray

1. Trim fat from tenderloins; place tenderloins in a large shallow dish. Combine soy sauce, ginger, and garlic; stir well. Pour soy sauce mixture over tenderloins. Cover and marinate in refrigerator 1 hour, turning tenderloins occasionally.

2. Preheat oven to 375°.

3. Remove tenderloins from dish; discard marinade. Pat tenderloins dry with paper towels. Brush tenderloins with honey, and roll in sesame seeds. Place tenderloins on a broiler pan coated with cooking spray. Bake pork at 375° for 25 minutes or until an instant-read thermometer registers 160° (slightly pink). Let stand 5 minutes before slicing. Yield: 6 servings (serving size: 3 ounces).

POINTS: 5; **Diabetic Exchanges:** 3½ V-L Meat, 1 Starch, 1 Fat
Per serving: CAL 239 (26% from fat); PRO 27g; FAT 7g (sat 2g); CARB 17.4g; FIB 0.2g; CHOL 74mg; IRON 22mg; SOD 281mg; CALC 2mg

Artichoke-Pepper Pizza With Feta Cheese

1   teaspoon olive oil
1   cup red bell pepper strips
1   cup orange bell pepper strips
2   garlic cloves, minced and divided
¼   cup light mayonnaise
⅛ to ¼ teaspoon crushed red pepper
⅛   teaspoon black pepper
1   (9-ounce) package frozen artichoke hearts,
      thawed and drained
1   (1-pound) package Italian cheese-flavored
      pizza crust (such as Boboli)
½   cup (2 ounces) crumbled feta cheese
½   teaspoon dried thyme

1. Preheat oven to 450°.

2. Heat oil in a nonstick skillet over medium-high heat. Add bell pepper strips; sauté 3 minutes. Add half of minced garlic; sauté 1 minute. Remove from heat; set aside.

3. Place remaining half of garlic, mayonnaise, and next 3 ingredients in a food processor; process until finely chopped.

4. Place pizza crust on a baking sheet. Spread artichoke mixture over pizza crust, leaving a ½-inch border; top with bell pepper mixture. Sprinkle with feta cheese and thyme. Bake at 450° for 14 minutes or until crust is crisp (cheese will not melt). Yield: 6 servings (serving size: 1 wedge).

POINTS: 6; **Diabetic Exchanges:** 3 Starch, 1 Veg, 1 Fat
Per serving: CAL 311 (21% from fat); PRO 10.5g; FAT 7.2g (sat 3g); CARB 49.4g; FIB 2.5g; CHOL 12mg; IRON 2.4mg; SOD 710mg; CALC 121mg

Turkey Piccata

1   tablespoon lemon juice
4   (2-ounce) turkey breast cutlets
1½ tablespoons all-purpose flour
½   teaspoon paprika
¼   teaspoon white pepper
Cooking spray
½   teaspoon olive oil
¼   cup dry white wine
1   tablespoon lemon juice
1   tablespoon capers
1½ teaspoons chopped fresh parsley

1. Drizzle 1 tablespoon lemon juice over cutlets; set aside. Combine flour, paprika, and pepper in a shallow dish; dredge cutlets in flour mixture.

2. Coat a large nonstick skillet with cooking spray; add oil, and place over medium-high heat until hot. Add cutlets, and cook 2 minutes on each side or until browned. Place cutlets on a platter; set aside, and keep warm.

3. Add wine, 1 tablespoon lemon juice, and capers to skillet; cook 1 minute, stirring constantly. Pour over cutlets; sprinkle with parsley. Yield: 2 servings.

POINTS: 4; **Diabetic Exchanges:** 3½ V-L Meat, ½ Starch
Per serving: CAL 154 (11% from fat); PRO 26.4g; FAT 1.9g (sat 0.4g); CARB 6.8g; FIB 0.4g; CHOL 71mg; IRON 1.9mg; SOD 205mg; CALC 18mg

Artichoke-Pepper Pizza With Feta Cheese

Beef Stew

Sweet Potato Biscuits

These biscuits make great use of leftover sweet potatoes.

2 cups self-rising flour
¼ cup sugar
3 tablespoons vegetable shortening
2 tablespoons chilled butter or stick
   margarine, cut into small pieces
1 cup mashed cooked sweet potato or
   canned mashed sweet potato
⅓ cup whole milk
Cooking spray

1. Preheat oven to 400°.

2. Combine flour and sugar in a medium bowl; cut in shortening and butter with a pastry blender or 2 knives until mixture is crumbly. Add sweet potato and milk, stirring just until moist. Turn dough out onto a lightly floured surface, and knead 4 or 5 times.

3. Roll dough to a ½-inch thickness on a lightly floured surface; cut with a 2-inch biscuit cutter. Place biscuits on baking sheets coated with cooking spray. Reroll dough, if necessary.

4. Bake biscuits at 400° for 14 minutes or until lightly browned. Serve warm. Yield: 1½ dozen (serving size: 1 biscuit).

POINTS: 2; **Diabetic Exchanges**: 1 Starch, ½ Fat
Per serving: CAL 106 (29% from fat); PRO 1.8g; FAT 3.4g (sat 1.5g); CARB 17.7g; FIB 0.5g; CHOL 4mg; IRON 0.8mg; SOD 194mg; CALC 57mg

Beef Stew

Cooking spray
2 tablespoons vegetable oil
3 pounds beef stew meat, cut into
   1-inch pieces
1 cup chopped onion
¾ cup chopped celery
2 teaspoons salt, divided
½ teaspoon pepper
2 garlic cloves, minced
¾ cup all-purpose flour
2 cups water, divided
4 small onions, quartered
3 carrots, peeled and cut into 2-inch pieces
6 small round red potatoes, halved
1 cup dry red wine
1 cup chopped fresh tomato

1 tablespoon chopped fresh parsley
¼ teaspoon dried thyme
2 bay leaves

1. Coat a large Dutch oven with cooking spray; add oil, and place over medium-high heat until hot. Add meat, and cook until browned. Drain, and return to pan. Add chopped onion, celery, 1 teaspoon salt, pepper, and garlic; sauté until vegetables are tender.

2. Place flour in a small bowl. Gradually add 1 cup water, stirring with a whisk until well blended. Combine flour mixture, meat mixture, onion quarters, carrot pieces, and potato halves in a 4-quart electric slow cooker.

3. Combine remaining 1 teaspoon salt, remaining 1 cup water, wine, and next 4 ingredients; pour over meat mixture. Cover with lid; cook on high-heat setting for 5 hours or until meat and vegetables are tender. Discard bay leaves. Yield: 12 servings (serving size: about 1 cup).

Note: If you prefer a longer cooking time, cook on high-heat setting for 1 hour, then cook on low-heat setting for 8½ hours.

POINTS: 5; **Diabetic Exchanges**: 2½ L Meat, 1 Starch, 2 Veg
Per serving: CAL 281 (23% from fat); PRO 29.9g; FAT 7g (sat 1.9g); CARB 25.8g; FIB 3.6g; CHOL 44mg; IRON 4.5mg; SOD 478mg; CALC 54mg

Succotash

10 ears fresh corn
6   cups shelled fresh lima beans
Boiling water
3½ teaspoons salt

1. Place corn in a large Dutch oven, and cover with water. Bring to a boil, and cook 5 minutes. Remove from heat; drain and let cool. Cut kernels from ears of corn.

2. Cook beans, uncovered, in boiling water to cover 5 minutes. Drain, reserving liquid.

3. Combine corn kernels and beans in a bowl; stir well. Pack mixture into hot jars, filling to 1 inch from top. Bring bean liquid to a boil; pour into jars, filling to 1 inch from top (add additional

boiling water, if necessary). Add ½ teaspoon salt to each pint jar and 1 teaspoon salt to each quart jar. Remove air bubbles; wipe jar rims. Cover at once with metal lids, and screw on bands. Process in pressure canner at 10 pounds pressure (240°). Process pints for 1 hour and quarts for 1 hour and 25 minutes. Yield: 7 pints or 3½ quarts (serving size: ¼ cup).

High Altitude Additions: If you live in a high altitude area of over 1,000 feet above sea level, processing times will increase. Check canning guide books for times specific to your area.

POINTS: 0; **Diabetic Exchanges:** ½ Starch
Per serving: CAL 30 (0% from fat); PRO 1.6g; FAT 0g (sat 0g); CARB 6.7g; FIB 1.3g; CHOL 0mg; IRON 0.6mg; SOD 150mg; CALC 6mg

Sirloin-Vegetable Kabobs

2   pounds sirloin steak
½   cup dry sherry
½   cup soy sauce
3   tablespoons sugar
3   tablespoons white vinegar
½   teaspoon garlic powder
½   teaspoon salt
½   teaspoon pepper
2   small red onions, each cut into 8 wedges
1   (8-ounce) package fresh mushrooms
2   medium green bell peppers, cut into
    1-inch squares
1   small pineapple, peeled, cored, and cut
    into 1-inch chunks
2   cups cherry tomatoes
Cooking spray

1. Trim fat from sirloin steak; cut steak into 1-inch cubes.

2. Combine sherry and next 6 ingredients in a large shallow dish; stir well. Add steak cubes, stirring to coat. Cover and marinate in refrigerator 2 hours, stirring occasionally. Remove steak cubes from dish, reserving marinade.

3. Thread steak cubes, onion wedges, mushrooms, bell pepper squares, and pineapple chunks alternately onto 6 (10- or 12-inch) skewers. Thread tomatoes onto 2 (10- or 12-inch) skewers. Set aside.

4. Prepare grill. Place steak kabobs on grill rack coated with cooking spray; cover and grill 10 minutes or until desired degree of doneness, turning kabobs and basting occasionally with reserved marinade. Place tomato kabobs on grill rack; cover and grill 3 minutes. Yield: 6 servings.

POINTS: 7; **Diabetic Exchanges:** 5 V-L Meat, 2 Veg, 1½ Fat, ½ Fruit
Per serving: CAL 320 (23% from fat); PRO 37.5g; FAT 8.3g (sat 3.1g); CARB 18.7g; FIB 2.4g; CHOL 101mg; IRON 5.4mg; SOD 1,385mg; CALC 34mg

S K E W E R I N G   K A B O B S :

Alternately thread beef cubes and vegetable chunks onto skewers. To be sure kabobs cook evenly, don't crowd the pieces on the skewers.

Parmesan-Breaded Tofu Marinara

2   (10.5-ounce) packages extra-firm tofu,
    drained and cut into 1-inch cubes
1   tablespoon lemon juice
⅓   cup cornstarch
¼   cup grated Parmesan cheese
¼   cup dry breadcrumbs
1   tablespoon minced fresh parsley
1   teaspoon dried Italian seasoning
3   large egg whites
Cooking spray
4   cups hot cooked linguine (about 8 ounces
    uncooked pasta), cooked without salt or
    fat
2   cups bottled marinara sauce
1   tablespoon capers
Lemon wedges (optional)

1. Place tofu cubes and lemon juice in a large zip-top plastic bag; seal bag, and shake gently to coat. Add cornstarch to bag; seal bag, and shake gently to coat. Let stand 1 hour.

2. Combine Parmesan cheese, breadcrumbs, parsley, and Italian seasoning in another large zip-top plastic bag; seal bag, and shake well. Place egg whites in a shallow dish or pie plate; stir well. Remove tofu cubes from bag; discard cornstarch mixture. Place tofu cubes into egg whites; stir gently. Drain. Add tofu cubes to cheese mixture in bag; seal bag, and shake gently to coat.

3. Coat a large nonstick skillet with cooking spray, and place over medium heat until hot. Add tofu cubes, and cook 8 minutes or until browned, turning occasionally.

4. Spoon pasta onto plates; top with tofu cubes. Spoon marinara sauce over tofu and pasta; sprinkle with capers. Serve with lemon wedges, if desired. Yield: 4 servings (serving size: 1 cup pasta, 1 cup tofu, ½ cup marinara sauce, and ¾ teaspoon capers).

POINTS: 10; **Diabetic Exchanges:** 4 Starch, 2 Veg, 1½ V-L Meat, 1½ Fat
Per serving: CAL 495 (27% from fat); PRO 26.1g; FAT 14.6g (sat 2.9g); CARB 69.2g; FIB 5.2g; CHOL 4mg; IRON 11.9mg; SOD 1,229mg; CALC 287mg

Grilled Asian Chicken Salad

4   (4-ounce) skinned, boned chicken breast halves
Cooking spray
1   (3-ounce) package ramen noodles
1   tablespoon sesame seeds
½   cup white wine vinegar
⅓   cup honey
2   tablespoons hoisin sauce
1   tablespoon dark sesame oil
6   cups mixed baby salad greens
4   cups thinly sliced napa (Chinese) cabbage
2   cups seeded chopped yellow tomato
2   cups seeded chopped tomato
½   cup chopped fresh cilantro
Cilantro sprigs (optional)

1. Prepare grill. Place chicken on grill rack coated with cooking spray; cover and grill 6 minutes on each side or until done. Diagonally slice; set aside.

2. Preheat oven to 350°.

3. Crumble noodles into a 9-inch round cake pan; discard seasoning packet. Add sesame seeds to pan. Bake at 350° for 5 minutes or until lightly browned, stirring once. Let cool; set aside.

4. Combine vinegar and next 3 ingredients in a bowl; stir well. Remove and reserve ⅓ cup dressing; set aside. Add chicken to dressing in bowl; stir well. Cover and chill at least 1 hour.

5. Combine ramen noodle mixture, salad greens, cabbage, tomatoes, and chopped cilantro in a large bowl; toss well. Drizzle reserved ⅓ cup dressing over salad; toss well. Place about 2 cups salad on each of 6 plates; top evenly with chicken. Garnish with cilantro sprigs, if desired. Yield: 6 servings.

POINTS: 6; **Diabetic Exchanges:** 4 Veg, ½ Starch, 1½ V-L Meat, 2 Fat
Per serving: CAL 291 (28% from fat); PRO 21g; FAT 8.9g (sat 1.2g); CARB 28.1g; FIB 2.5g; CHOL 48mg; IRON 1.9mg; SOD 158mg; CALC 67mg

Stained Glass Salad

This sparkling gelatin salad will add color to your menu.

1½ cups water
2   (3-ounce) packages sparkling white grape-flavored or lemon-flavored gelatin
2   cups ginger ale, chilled

Toasting the ramen noodles and sesame seeds imparts a nutty taste and crunchy texture to Grilled Asian Chicken Salad.

1 cup seedless red grapes
1 (11-ounce) can mandarin oranges in light syrup, drained
1 (8-ounce) can pineapple tidbits, drained
Cooking spray
Curly leaf lettuce leaves (optional)
Seedless red grape clusters (optional)

1. Bring water to a boil in a small saucepan. Add gelatin; cook 2 minutes or until gelatin dissolves, stirring constantly. Pour into a large bowl; chill 15 minutes. Gently stir in chilled ginger ale. Cover and chill 1 hour or until consistency of un-beaten egg white. Gently stir 15 seconds. Stir in 1 cup grapes, oranges, and pineapple.

2. Pour mixture into a 6-cup decorative mold coated with cooking spray. Cover and chill until firm or up to 3 days. Unmold salad onto a lettuce-lined serving plate, and garnish with grape clusters, if desired. Yield: 8 servings.

POINTS: 3; **Diabetic Exchanges:** 2 Starch
Per serving: CAL 150 (0% from fat); PRO 2.1g; FAT 0.2g (sat 0g); CARB 35.8g; FIB 0.7g; CHOL 0mg; IRON 0.4mg; SOD 88mg; CALC 12mg

Chicken-Fried Wild Rice has a chewier texture and nuttier flavor than the traditional dish made with white rice.

Chicken-Fried Wild Rice

1 pound skinned, boned chicken breasts, cut into 1-inch pieces
¼ cup low-salt teriyaki sauce
¼ cup low-salt soy sauce
¼ cup dry white wine
½ teaspoon peeled grated fresh ginger
¼ teaspoon Chinese five-spice powder
2 garlic cloves, minced
1 teaspoon vegetable oil
1 cup green bell pepper strips
⅔ cup sliced carrot
⅔ cup chopped onion
⅔ cup sliced fresh mushrooms
½ cup frozen green peas, thawed
1¾ cups hot cooked wild rice (1 [4-ounce] package), cooked without salt or fat
Cooking spray
2 tablespoons slivered almonds, toasted

1. Combine first 7 ingredients in a bowl; stir well. Cover and marinate in refrigerator at least 1 hour.

2. Heat oil in a wok or nonstick skillet over medium-high heat. Add bell pepper, carrot, and onion; stir-fry 3 minutes. Add mushrooms and peas; stir-fry 2 minutes. Spoon vegetable mixture into a large bowl. Stir in rice; set aside.

3. Coat wok or skillet with cooking spray; place over medium-high heat until hot. Add chicken and marinade, and stir-fry 4 minutes or until chicken is done. Add rice mixture; stir-fry 2 minutes or until thoroughly heated. Sprinkle with almonds. Yield: 4 servings (serving size: 1½ cups).

POINTS: 6; **Diabetic Exchanges:** 3½ V-L Meat, 2 Starch, 1 Veg
Per serving: CAL 322 (14% from fat); PRO 33.5g; FAT 4.9g (sat 1.6g); CARB 33.7g; FIB 3.7g; CHOL 66mg; IRON 2.7mg; SOD 754mg; CALC 49mg

Pepper-Crusted Venison Tenderloin

Cola as a marinade mellows the sometimes gamey taste of venison. Then this recipe brings on horseradish, cracked pepper, and coarse-grained mustard to ensure memorable flavor.

2 (1-pound) venison tenderloins
1 (12-ounce) can cola
¼ cup coarse-grained mustard
2 tablespoons coarsely ground or cracked pepper
Cooking spray

½ cup red currant jelly, melted
2 tablespoons prepared horseradish
1 tablespoon coarse-grained mustard

1. Preheat oven to 450°.

2. Place tenderloins and cola in a large zip-top plastic bag; seal bag, and marinate in refrigerator 2 hours. Remove tenderloins from bag; discard marinade. Spread ¼ cup mustard evenly over top and sides of tenderloins; pat pepper into mustard. Place tenderloins on a broiler pan coated with cooking spray. Bake at 450° for 15 minutes. Reduce oven temperature to 350°, and bake an additional 40 minutes or until an instant-read thermometer registers 160° (medium). Let stand 10 minutes before slicing.

3. Combine jelly, horseradish, and 1 tablespoon mustard; stir well. Serve with venison. Yield: 8 servings (serving size: 3 ounces venison and 1½ tablespoons sauce).

POINTS: 5; **Diabetic Exchanges:** 3½ V-L Meat, 1 Starch
Per serving: CAL 156 (22% from fat); PRO 26.5g; FAT 3.8g (sat 1.1g); CARB 19.6g; FIB 0.5g; CHOL 95mg; IRON 4.4mg; SOD 329mg; CALC 28mg

Creamy Ham-and-Chicken Lasagna

2 (6-ounce) skinned chicken breast halves (bone-in)
2 cups chopped lean ham
Cooking spray
1 (8-ounce) package sliced fresh mushrooms
2 tablespoons butter or stick margarine
⅓ cup all-purpose flour
3 cups fat-free milk
1½ cups (6 ounces) shredded fresh Parmesan cheese
2 teaspoons chopped fresh or ¾ teaspoon dried basil
½ teaspoon salt
¼ teaspoon freshly ground pepper
9 cooked lasagna noodles, cooked without salt or fat
Chopped fresh parsley (optional)
Paprika (optional)

1. Place chicken breasts in a saucepan; add water to cover. Bring to a boil; cover, reduce heat to medium, and cook 45 minutes or until chicken is tender. Drain; let cool slightly. Remove chicken from bones, and chop into bite-size pieces. Combine chicken and ham in a bowl; set aside.

2. Preheat oven to 350°.

3. Coat a large nonstick skillet with cooking spray; place over medium-high heat until hot. Add mushrooms; sauté until tender. Drain; add to chicken mixture in bowl.

4. Melt 2 tablespoons butter in skillet over medium-high heat. Add flour, and cook 1 minute, stirring constantly. Gradually stir in milk; cook 3 minutes, stirring constantly. Add cheese and next 3 ingredients; cook until cheese melts and sauce is thick, stirring constantly. Add chicken mixture to sauce; stir well.

5. Coat a 13- x 9-inch baking dish with cooking spray. Spread one-fourth of chicken-sauce mixture into bottom of dish; top with 3 lasagna noodles. Repeat layers with remaining chicken-sauce mixture and noodles, ending with chicken-sauce mixture.

6. Cover and bake at 350° for 40 minutes or until thoroughly heated. Let stand 10 minutes before serving. Garnish with parsley and paprika, if desired. Yield: 8 servings.

POINTS: 8; **Diabetic Exchanges:** 2 V-L Meat, 1½ Wh Milk, ½ Starch
Per serving: CAL 337 (36% from fat); PRO 26.4g; FAT 13.3g (sat 7.1g); CARB 27.6g; FIB 1.1g; CHOL 77mg; IRON 2mg; SOD 1,066mg; CALC 419mg

Sweet-and-Sour Green Beans

1 pound fresh green beans, trimmed
Cooking spray
¾ cup thinly sliced onion, separated into rings
1 (4-ounce) jar sliced pimiento, undrained
¼ cup cider vinegar
1 tablespoon extra-virgin olive oil
2 tablespoons sugar
1 teaspoon salt

1. Cook green beans in boiling water to cover 6 minutes or until crisp-tender; drain. Rinse under cold water; drain and set aside.

2. Coat a large nonstick skillet with cooking spray; place over medium heat until hot. Add onion; sauté 5 minutes or until tender. Remove from heat; set aside.

3. Drain pimiento, reserving liquid. Set sliced pimiento aside. Combine reserved pimiento liquid, vinegar, and next 3 ingredients in a small bowl, stirring with a whisk until blended. Set dressing aside.

4. Combine beans, onion, and pimiento in a large bowl. Add dressing; toss gently to coat. Serve at room temperature, or cover and chill 2 hours. Serve with a slotted spoon. Yield: 4 servings (serving size: about 1 cup).

Note: You can substitute 2 (9-ounce) packages frozen whole green beans cooked without salt for fresh green beans, if desired.

POINTS: 2; **Diabetic Exchanges:** 2 Veg, ½ Starch, ½ Fat
Per serving: CAL 108 (30% from fat); PRO 2.7g; FAT 3.6g (sat 0.5g); CARB 18.9g; FIB 2.9g; CHOL 0mg; IRON 1.8mg; SOD 598mg; CALC 50mg

Eggplant-Sausage-Pasta Casserole

2   pounds turkey Italian sausage
Cooking spray
6   cups peeled (½-inch) cubed eggplant
        (about 1½ pounds)
1   cup chopped onion
2   garlic cloves, minced
2   teaspoons paprika
1   (28-ounce) can crushed tomatoes,
        undrained
1   (6-ounce) can tomato paste
1   tablespoon dried Italian seasoning
1   teaspoon dried basil
¾   teaspoon salt
½   teaspoon crushed red pepper
8½   cups cooked penne pasta (about 16 ounces
        uncooked tubular pasta), cooked without
        salt or fat
1   (15-ounce) container fat-free ricotta cheese
3   cups (12 ounces) shredded part-skim
        mozzarella cheese, divided

1. Remove sausage from casings. Brown sausage in a large nonstick skillet coated with cooking spray over medium heat, stirring to crumble. Drain well; return to skillet. Add eggplant, onion, and garlic; sauté over medium heat 8 minutes or until eggplant is tender. Add paprika; sauté 1 minute. Add tomatoes and next 5 ingredients; bring to a boil, stirring occasionally. Reduce heat, and simmer, uncovered, 20 minutes, stirring occasionally. Stir in pasta. Remove from heat, and let cool.

2. Preheat oven to 350°.

3. Divide half of eggplant mixture evenly between 2 (11- x 7-inch) baking dishes. Divide ricotta cheese evenly between dishes, and spread gently over eggplant mixture; sprinkle each casserole with ¾ cup mozzarella cheese. Spread remaining half of eggplant mixture evenly over each casserole.

4. Bake at 350° for 30 minutes. Sprinkle each casserole with ¾ cup mozzarella cheese; bake an additional 5 minutes. Yield: 2 casseroles, 6 servings each.

Note: You can assemble the casseroles ahead of time, omitting the mozzarella cheese from the top of each casserole; cover and freeze up to 6 months (thaw frozen casseroles overnight in refrigerator). Bake at 350° for 45 minutes or until bubbly. Sprinkle each casserole with ¾ cup mozzarella cheese, and bake an additional 5 minutes.

POINTS: 8; **Diabetic Exchanges:** 2½ L Meat, 2 Starch, 1 Sk Milk
Per serving: CAL 399 (26% from fat); PRO 30.2g; FAT 11.5g (sat 0.2g); CARB 43.8g; FIB 3.1g; CHOL 41.2mg; IRON 4.1mg; SOD 833mg; CALC 353mg

SHREDDING CHEESE:

When recipes specify shredding an ingredient like cheese, use the largest holes of an upright grater. It will yield long shreds.

Chutney-Glazed Apples

If you're not a curry fan, omit the curry and you'll still have a delicious apple side dish.

2½ pounds Granny Smith apples, peeled, cored, and cut into ½-inch wedges
Cooking spray
⅓ cup orange marmalade
⅓ cup mango chutney
2 tablespoons butter or stick margarine
1 teaspoon ground cinnamon
½ teaspoon curry powder

1. Preheat oven to 400°.

2. Arrange apple wedges in an 11- x 7-inch baking dish coated with cooking spray; set aside.

3. Combine marmalade and next 4 ingredients in a small saucepan; bring to a boil over medium heat, stirring constantly. Pour over apple wedges; toss well. Bake at 400° for 25 minutes or until tender. Yield: 8 servings.

POINTS: 2; **Diabetic Exchanges:** 2½ Fruit, ½ Fat
Per serving: CAL 167 (17% from fat); PRO 0.4g; FAT 3.1g (sat 1.9g); CARB 37.2g; FIB 2.8g; CHOL 8mg; IRON 0.4mg; SOD 150mg; CALC 19mg

Baked Mushroom Rice

2 tablespoons butter or stick margarine
3 cups chicken or beef broth
¾ cup sliced green onions
½ cup dry sherry
1 teaspoon seasoned or black pepper
¾ teaspoon salt
1 (4½-ounce) jar sliced mushrooms, undrained
1 (4-ounce) jar diced pimiento, drained
2 cups uncooked long-grain rice
Cooking spray

1. Preheat oven to 375°.

2. Melt butter in a large nonstick skillet over high heat. Add broth and next 6 ingredients; bring to a boil. Remove from heat; stir in rice. Spoon into a 13- x 9-inch baking dish coated with cooking spray. Cover and bake at 375° for 25 minutes or until liquid is absorbed and rice is tender. Stir before serving. Yield: 8 servings (serving size: about 1 cup).

POINTS: 4; **Diabetic Exchanges:** 2½ Starch, ½ Fat
Per serving: CAL 219 (16% from fat); PRO 5.8g; FAT 3.8g (sat 2g); CARB 39.3g; FIB 1g; CHOL 8mg; IRON 2.7mg; SOD 756mg; CALC 27mg

Stewed Tomato Bake

2 (14½-ounce) cans stewed tomatoes, undrained
1½ tablespoons cornstarch
Cooking spray
1¼ teaspoons dried basil
½ teaspoon dried marjoram
½ teaspoon freshly ground pepper
10 round buttery crackers, crushed
3 tablespoons grated Parmesan cheese

1. Preheat oven to 450°.

2. Drain tomatoes, reserving juice. Combine reserved juice and cornstarch in a bowl; stir with a whisk until well blended. Pour juice mixture into a 1-quart baking dish coated with cooking spray. Stir in tomatoes, basil, marjoram, and pepper. Bake at 450° for 15 minutes. Remove from oven, and stir gently. Combine cracker crumbs and cheese; sprinkle evenly over tomato mixture. Bake an additional 5 minutes or until lightly browned. Yield: 4 servings (serving size: 1 cup).

POINTS: 3; **Diabetic Exchanges:** 1½ Veg, ½ Starch, ½ Sk Milk, ½ Fat
Per serving: CAL 141 (29% from fat); PRO 4.1g; FAT 4.5g (sat 1g); CARB 21.6g; FIB 1.1g; CHOL 3mg; IRON 2.2mg; SOD 664mg; CALC 139mg

Chutney-Glazed Apples are a highly-flavored side dish for pork or ham.

One Last Course

THERE'S ALWAYS TIME—
AND ROOM—FOR DESSERT.

*I*t's a well-known phenomenon: No matter how satisfied you are at the end of a meal, it seems you're hungry all over again when dessert is brought out. It's as if your appetite for sweets occupies a separate part of your brain—the part that wants to celebrate, splurge, and linger.

But then worry creeps in: How many grams of fat does it have? Can I afford the extra **POINTS?** How much exercise will it take to burn it off? The occasional indulgence shouldn't cause you inner turmoil. A healthy attitude toward eating leaves room for enjoying sweets without feeling guilty. So get reacquainted with your sweet tooth—a number of these recipes are relatively low in **POINTS.** You'll be perfectly justified.

Plump, sugar-capped dumplings sit atop sweet, spiced fruit in this old-fashioned Apple Cobbler.

Apple Cobbler

4   cups peeled, thinly sliced Granny Smith
    apple (about 4 large apples)
⅔ cup sugar, divided
⅓ cup orange juice
1   tablespoon cornstarch
½ teaspoon ground cinnamon
¼ teaspoon ground nutmeg
1   cup all-purpose flour
1½ teaspoons baking powder
¼ teaspoon salt
¼ cup chilled butter or stick margarine, cut
    into small pieces
½ cup fat-free milk
2   teaspoons sugar

1. Preheat oven to 375°.

2. Combine apple slices, ⅓ cup sugar, orange juice, and next 3 ingredients in a large bowl; toss gently to coat. Spoon mixture into an 11- x 7-inch baking dish.

3. Combine remaining ⅓ cup sugar, flour, baking powder, and salt in a bowl; cut in butter with a pastry blender or 2 knives until mixture resembles coarse meal. Add milk; stir with a fork just until moist.

4. Drop dough into 8 mounds on top of apple mixture; sprinkle 2 teaspoons sugar over dough. Bake at 375° for 35 minutes or until dumplings are golden brown. Serve warm or at room temperature. Yield: 8 servings.

POINTS: 5; **Diabetic Exchanges:** 2 Starch, 1 Fruit, 1 Fat
Per serving: CAL 236 (23% from fat); PRO 2g; FAT 6g (sat 1.2g) CARB 44g; FIB 2.6g; CHOL 0mg; IRON 1mg; SOD 223mg; CALC 80mg

Bread Pudding With Whiskey Sauce

5   cups (1-inch) cubed French bread
2   cups evaporated fat-free milk
½ cup egg substitute
⅓ cup firmly packed brown sugar
1¼ teaspoons ground cinnamon
1   teaspoon ground nutmeg
1½ teaspoons vanilla extract
⅓ cup raisins
Butter-flavored cooking spray
Whiskey Sauce

1. Preheat oven to 350°.

2. Place bread cubes on a baking sheet; bake at 350° for 15 minutes or until toasted.

3. Combine milk and next 5 ingredients in a large bowl; stir well with a whisk. Add bread and raisins; toss well. Divide mixture evenly among 8 (6-ounce) ramekins or custard cups coated with cooking spray.

4. Place cups in a baking pan; add hot water to pan to a depth of ¾ inch. Bake at 350° for 30 minutes or until a knife inserted in center comes out clean. Spoon 2 tablespoons Whiskey Sauce over each pudding. Serve pudding warm. Yield: 8 servings.

POINTS: 4; **Diabetic Exchanges:** 2½ Starch
Per serving: CAL 212 (8% from fat); PRO 8g; FAT 2g (sat 0.4g) CARB 37g; FIB 0.7g; CHOL 3mg; IRON 1.4mg; SOD 234mg; CALC 227mg

Whiskey Sauce:

¾ cup water
¼ cup whiskey or bourbon
2   tablespoons granulated sugar
1   tablespoon cornstarch
1   tablespoon reduced-calorie stick margarine

Presented in individual baking cups, Bread Pudding With Whiskey Sauce is the ideal dessert to serve at a dinner gathering.

1. Combine all ingredients in a small saucepan; bring to a boil over medium heat, and cook 1 minute, stirring constantly. Serve sauce warm. Yield: 1 cup.

Black Bottom Cranberry Pudding

⅔ cup chocolate wafer crumbs (about 12 wafers, such as Nabisco Famous Chocolate Wafers)
2 tablespoons reduced-calorie stick margarine, melted
¾ cup granulated sugar, divided
6 tablespoons water
2 cups fresh or frozen cranberries, thawed
¼ cup seedless raspberry jam
1 cup 1% low-fat milk
2 large egg yolks
¼ cup all-purpose flour
5 large egg whites (at room temperature)
1 teaspoon powdered sugar

1. Combine wafer crumbs and margarine in a bowl; stir well. Press crumb mixture into bottom of an 8-inch square baking pan; set aside.

2. Combine 6 tablespoons granulated sugar and water in a medium saucepan; bring to a boil over medium heat. Add cranberries, and return to a boil. Reduce heat, and simmer, uncovered, 10 minutes, stirring occasionally. Remove from heat; stir in jam. Let cool. Spoon cranberry mixture into prepared pan.

3. Place milk in a small saucepan; bring just to a boil over medium heat, stirring occasionally. Remove from heat; keep warm. Beat ¼ cup granulated sugar and egg yolks at high speed of a mixer until thick and pale (about 5 minutes). Gently stir flour into yolk mixture using a whisk. Gradually stir about ¼ cup hot milk into yolk mixture; add to remaining hot milk, stirring constantly. Place over medium-low heat, and cook 1 minute or until thick, stirring constantly. Pour into a large bowl; let cool.

4. Preheat oven to 375°.

5. Beat egg whites at high speed of a mixer until soft peaks form. Gradually add remaining 2 tablespoons granulated sugar, beating until stiff peaks form. Stir one fourth of egg white mixture into cooled milk mixture; fold in remaining egg white mixture. Pour egg mixture over cranberry mixture in pan. Bake at 375° for 20 minutes or until puffed and golden. Sprinkle with powdered sugar. Serve immediately. Yield: 8 servings.

POINTS: 5; **Diabetic Exchanges:** 2 Starch, ½ Fruit, ½ Fat
Per serving: CAL 210 (21% from fat); PRO 5g; FAT 5g (sat 1.3g); CARB 36g; FIB 0.5g; CHOL 62mg; IRON 0.6mg; SOD 113mg; CALC 58mg

Buttered Rum Milk Shakes

3 cups butter pecan crunch low-fat ice cream (such as Healthy Choice)
2 cups ice cubes
½ cup fat-free milk
1 tablespoon dark rum

1. Combine all ingredients in a blender, and process until smooth. Serve immediately. Yield: 4 servings (serving size: 1 cup).

POINTS: 4; **Diabetic Exchanges:** 2 Starch, ½ Sk Milk
Per serving: Calories 199 (14% from fat); PRO 6g; Fat 3g (sat 1.5g); CARB 35g; FIB 1.5g; CHOL 1mg; IRON 0mg; SOD 106mg; CALC 187mg

Pineapple Sherbet

3 cups whole milk
¾ cup half-and-half
⅓ cup sugar
2 tablespoons fresh lemon juice
1 (15¼-ounce) can crushed pineapple in juice, undrained
1 (12-ounce) can frozen pineapple juice concentrate, thawed and undiluted

1. Combine all ingredients in a large bowl; stir with a whisk until sugar dissolves.

2. Pour mixture into the freezer can of an ice cream freezer; freeze according to manufacturer's instructions. Spoon sherbet into a freezer-safe container; cover and freeze 1 hour or until firm. Yield: 19 servings (serving size: ½ cup).

POINTS: 2; **Diabetic Exchanges:** 1 Fruit, ½ Fat
Per serving: CAL 96 (28% from fat); PRO 2g; FAT 3g (sat 1.5g); CARB 18g; FIB 0.3g; CHOL 9mg; IRON 0.2mg; SOD 24mg; CALC 61mg

Caramel-Brownie Chunk Ice Cream

Save the remaining brownie mix to make this dessert again or use it to make a half-batch of brownies (see our note following the recipe).

1   (14-ounce) can low-fat sweetened condensed milk
½   (1-pound, 4.5-ounce) package low-fat fudge brownie mix (about 2 cups)
¼   cup water
1   large egg white
Cooking spray
2   large egg yolks
¼   cup sugar
¼   cup all-purpose flour
3   cups 1% low-fat milk
2   (12-ounce) cans evaporated fat-free milk

1. Preheat oven to 425°.

2. Pour sweetened condensed milk into a 9-inch pie plate; cover with foil. Place pie plate in a large baking or roasting pan; add hot water to pan to a depth of ¼ inch. Bake at 425° for 1 hour and 20 minutes or until sweetened condensed milk is thick and caramel colored (add hot water to pan as needed). Remove foil; let caramelized milk cool. Decrease oven temperature to 350°.

3. Combine one-half package brownie mix, water, and egg white in a bowl; stir well. Spread into an 8-inch square baking pan coated with cooking spray. Bake at 350° for 20 minutes or just until done (do not overbake). Let cool on a wire rack.

4. Place egg yolks in a bowl; stir well with a whisk, and set aside. Combine sugar and flour in a large saucepan; stir well. Gradually add 1% low-fat milk and evaporated fat-free milk, stirring with a whisk until well blended. Place over medium heat, and cook 15 minutes or until thick, stirring constantly. Gradually stir one-fourth of hot mixture into egg yolks; add to remaining hot mixture, stirring constantly. Place over medium heat; cook 1 minute, stirring constantly. Remove from heat; stir in caramelized milk. Let cool. Chill thoroughly.

5. Pour mixture into the freezer can of an ice cream freezer; freeze according to manufacturer's instructions. Cut brownie into ½-inch cubes; stir into ice cream. Spoon ice cream into a freezer-safe container; cover and freeze 1 hour or until firm. Yield: 18 servings (serving size: ½ cup).

Note: Combine remaining brownie mix and ⅓ cup water; stir well. Spread into a 8-inch square baking pan coated with cooking spray. Bake at 350° for 25 minutes.

POINTS: 4; **Diabetic Exchanges:** 2 Starch, ½ Sk Milk
Per serving: CAL 203 (13% from fat); PRO 8g; FAT 3g (sat 1.3g); CARB 36g; FIB 0.5g; CHOL 30mg; IRON 0.6mg; SOD 145mg; CALC 207mg

Caramel-Kahlúa Squares

This sinfully delicious dessert received a top rating from our staff. We polished off every bite.

⅓   cup chocolate wafer crumbs (about 6 wafers, such as Nabisco Famous Chocolate Wafers)
2   teaspoons reduced-calorie stick margarine, melted
Cooking spray
6   cups vanilla low-fat ice cream, softened
2   tablespoons Kahlúa (coffee-flavored liqueur)
½   cup fat-free caramel-flavored sundae syrup
2   tablespoons strong brewed coffee

1. Combine wafer crumbs and margarine in a bowl; stir well. Sprinkle half of crumb mixture over bottom of an 8-inch square baking pan coated with cooking spray.

2. Combine ice cream and Kahlúa in a large bowl; stir well. Spread half of ice cream mixture into prepared pan. Combine caramel syrup and coffee in a small bowl; stir well. Drizzle half of caramel mixture over ice cream mixture; freeze until firm.

3. Spread remaining ice cream mixture over frozen caramel mixture, and drizzle with remaining caramel mixture. Sprinkle evenly with remaining crumb mixture; freeze until firm. Cut into 9 squares. Yield: 9 servings.

POINTS: 5; **Diabetic Exchanges:** 1½ Starch, 1 Fat, ½ Sk Milk
Per serving: CAL 206 (26% from fat); PRO 4g; FAT 6g (sat 2.5g); CARB 33g; FIB 0.2g; CHOL 11mg; IRON 4.1mg; SOD 104mg; CALC 161mg

Lemon Bars

Avoid the bitter white pith just below the yellow skin when grating lemon rind. One medium lemon yields about 1 tablespoon rind and about 2 tablespoons juice.

1   cup all-purpose flour
⅓   cup powdered sugar, divided
1   teaspoon grated lemon rind
5   tablespoons chilled reduced-calorie stick margarine, cut into small pieces
Cooking spray
1   cup granulated sugar
½   cup egg substitute
¼   cup fresh lemon juice

1. Preheat oven to 350°.

2. Combine flour, ¼ cup powdered sugar, and lemon rind in a bowl; cut in margarine with a pastry blender or 2 knives until mixture resembles coarse crumbs. Press mixture into a 9-inch square baking pan coated with cooking spray. Bake at 350° for 18 minutes.

3. Combine 1 cup granulated sugar, egg substitute, and lemon juice in a bowl; stir well with a whisk. Pour over baked crust. Bake at 350° for 25 minutes or until set. Let cool completely on a wire rack.

4. Sprinkle with remaining powdered sugar. Cut into 16 bars. Store in an airtight container. Yield: 16 servings.

POINTS: 3; **Diabetic Exchanges:** 1½ Starch
Per serving: CAL 122 (22% from fat); PRO 1g; FAT 3g (sat 0g); CARB 23g; FIB 0.2g; CHOL 0mg; IRON 0.5mg; SOD 34mg; CALC 4mg

Chewy Chocolate Cookies

1   (1 pound, 2.25-ounce) package reduced-fat devil's food cake mix
2   tablespoons butter or stick margarine, softened
2   tablespoons water
2   large egg whites
1   large egg
¾   cup semisweet chocolate chips
Cooking spray

1. Preheat oven to 350°.

2. Combine first 5 ingredients in a large bowl; beat at medium speed of a mixer 2 minutes. Stir in chocolate chips. Drop by rounded teaspoons 2 inches apart onto baking sheets coated with cooking spray. Bake at 350° for 10 minutes. Remove from pans; let cool on wire racks. Store in an airtight container. Yield: 5 dozen (serving size: 1 cookie).

POINTS: 1; **Diabetic Exchanges:** ½ Starch
Per serving: CAL 50 (27% from fat); PRO 0.7g; FAT 1.5g (sat 0.6g); CARB 8.4g; FIB 0.2g; CHOL 4mg; IRON 0.3mg; SOD 79mg; CALC 9mg

Caramel Swirl Ice Box Cake

21   ladyfingers, split and divided
3½   cups vanilla low-fat frozen yogurt, softened
¾   cup frozen reduced-calorie whipped topping, thawed
½   cup fat-free caramel-flavored sundae syrup, divided
1   (10-ounce) package frozen raspberries in light syrup, thawed and undrained

1. Line an 8½- x 4½-inch loaf pan with plastic wrap, smoothing plastic wrap in corners and on sides of pan. Arrange one-third of ladyfinger halves, cut sides up, on bottom of loaf pan, and, cut sides facing in, around sides of loaf pan; set aside.

2. Place yogurt in a large bowl; fold in whipped topping. Spoon half of yogurt mixture into prepared loaf pan. Spoon ¼ cup caramel syrup over yogurt mixture. Swirl caramel syrup with a knife to create a marbled effect. Arrange half of remaining ladyfinger halves on top of caramel. Repeat layers with remaining yogurt mixture, remaining ¼ cup caramel syrup, and remaining ladyfinger halves. Cover and freeze at least 8 hours.

3. Place a serving platter, upside down, on top of loaf pan; invert cake onto platter. Carefully remove plastic wrap. Cut cake into 10 slices. Top each slice evenly with raspberries and syrup. Yield: 10 servings.

POINTS: 4; **Diabetic Exchanges:** 1½ Starch, 1 Fruit, ½ Fat
Per serving: CAL 193 (14% from fat); PRO 4g; FAT 3g (sat 1.5g); CARB 39g; FIB 2.2g; CHOL 32mg; IRON 3.8mg; SOD 176mg; CALC 122mg

Lemon Bars

Chocolate Silk Cheesecake

Chocolate Silk Cheesecake

Using a food processor instead of a mixer makes this cheesecake creamier and smoother.

⅔ cup reduced-fat chocolate wafer crumbs (such as Nabisco Nilla)
2   tablespoons sugar
1   tablespoon butter or stick margarine, melted
1   tablespoon water
Cooking spray
½   cup semisweet chocolate chips
2   tablespoons fat-free milk
1¼ cups sugar
3   (8-ounce) blocks fat-free cream cheese
1   (8-ounce) block ⅓-less-fat cream cheese (Neufchâtel)
1   tablespoon vanilla extract
¼   teaspoon salt
4   large egg whites
1   cup 30%-less-fat sour cream (such as Breakstone)
½   cup Dutch process or unsweetened cocoa
½   cup hot fudge topping
2   cups frozen reduced-calorie whipped topping, thawed

1. Preheat oven to 400°.

2. Combine first 4 ingredients in a bowl; toss with a fork until blended. Press crumb mixture into bottom of a 9-inch springform pan coated with cooking spray. Bake at 400° for 8 minutes. Let cool on a wire rack. Increase oven temperature to 525°.

3. Combine chocolate chips and milk in a bowl; microwave at HIGH 45 seconds or until chocolate melts, stirring after 30 seconds. Let cool.

4. Combine 1¼ cups sugar, cheeses, vanilla, and salt in a food processor, and process just until smooth. Add egg whites; process just until blended. Add chocolate mixture, sour cream, cocoa, and fudge topping; process just until blended.

5. Spoon batter into prepared pan. Bake at 525° for 7 minutes. Reduce oven temperature to 250°, and bake 25 minutes or until almost set (cheesecake is done when the center barely moves when the pan is touched). Remove cheesecake from oven; run a knife around outside edge, and let cool to room temperature. Cover and chill at least 8 hours. Serve with whipped topping. Yield: 16 servings (serving size: 1 slice cheesecake and 2 tablespoons whipped topping).

POINTS: 6; Diabetic Exchanges: 2 Starch, 1 Fat, ½ Sk Milk
Per serving: CAL 279 (28% from fat); PRO 11g; FAT 9g (sat 4.7g); CARB 36g; FIB 0.1g; CHOL 26mg; IRON 0.9mg; SOD 455mg; CALC 161mg

Stirred Custard

The consistency of this dessert is similar to a pourable sauce.

3   cups whole milk
2   large eggs
⅔   cup sugar
1½ tablespoons all-purpose flour
1   teaspoon vanilla extract

1. Place milk in the top of a double boiler; cook over boiling water until milk is thoroughly heated. Set aside.

2. Place eggs in a medium bowl; beat at medium speed of a mixer until frothy. Add sugar and flour, beating until thick. Gradually stir about 1 cup hot milk into egg mixture; add to remaining hot mixture, stirring constantly.

3. Cook mixture in top of double boiler over low heat 30 minutes or until thick, stirring occasionally. Remove from heat; stir in vanilla. Serve warm or chilled. Yield: 6 servings (serving size: about ⅔ cup).

Note: When cooking custards and puddings in a saucepan, stir with a gentle figure 8 motion. This helps to ensure a smooth consistency with no lumps. Don't stir too vigorously, though, or you might break down the thickening.

POINTS: 4; Diabetic Exchanges: 1½ Starch, 1 Fat, ½ Sk Milk
Per serving: CAL 194 (28% from fat); PRO 7g; FAT 6g (sat 3.1g); CARB 30g; FIB 0.1g; CHOL 87mg; IRON 0.5mg; SOD 81mg; CALC 155mg

Pumpkin Flan

1   cup sugar, divided
1   (16-ounce) can unsweetened pumpkin
1   teaspoon pumpkin pie spice
1   teaspoon vanilla extract
½   teaspoon maple extract
1   (12-ounce) can evaporated fat-free milk

½ cup fat-free milk
¼ cup orange juice
2 large eggs, lightly beaten
2 large egg whites, lightly beaten
Cinnamon sticks (optional)
Orange rind curls (optional)

1. Preheat oven to 350°.

2. Place ½ cup sugar in a small, heavy saucepan. Place over medium heat, and cook until sugar dissolves, stirring frequently. Continue cooking until light brown, stirring constantly. Immediately pour into a 9-inch round cake pan, tilting quickly until caramelized sugar coats bottom of cake pan. Set aside.

3. Combine remaining ½ cup sugar, pumpkin, and next 3 ingredients in a bowl; stir well. Add milks, orange juice, eggs, and egg whites; stir well. Pour pumpkin mixture into prepared pan; place in a large shallow pan. Pour hot water into large pan to a depth of 1 inch. Bake at 350° for 1 hour and 5 minutes or until a knife inserted in center comes out clean. Remove cake pan from water, and let cool on a wire rack. Cover and chill at least 4 hours.

4. Loosen edges of flan with a knife or rubber spatula. Place a serving platter, upside down, on top of cake pan; invert onto platter. Drizzle any remaining caramelized syrup over flan. Garnish with cinnamon sticks and orange rind curls, if desired. Cut into wedges. Yield: 8 servings.

POINTS: 3; **Diabetic Exchanges:** 2 Starch, 1 Veg
Per serving: CAL 184 (10% from fat); PRO 7g; FAT 2g (sat 0.6g); CARB 36g; FIB 2.4g; CHOL 56mg; IRON 1.1mg; SOD 88mg; CALC 166mg

Mississippi Mud Brownies

1 (1-pound, 4.5-ounce) package low-fat fudge brownie mix
⅔ cup water
1 teaspoon vanilla extract
½ cup reduced-fat semisweet chocolate chips
Cooking spray
2 cups miniature marshmallows
1 (16-ounce) can reduced-fat chocolate-flavored frosting

1. Preheat oven to 350°.

2. Combine brownie mix, ⅔ cup water, and vanilla in a bowl; stir well. Stir in chocolate chips. Spread batter in a 13- x 9-inch baking pan coated with cooking spray. Bake at 350° for 23 minutes. Sprinkle marshmallows over hot brownies, and bake an additional 2 minutes. Let cool completely in pan on a wire rack. Spread frosting over brownies; let stand at least 30 minutes. Cut into 24 squares. Yield: 2 dozen (serving size: 1 brownie).

POINTS: 4; **Diabetic Exchanges:** 2½ Starch, 1 Fat
Per serving: CAL 208 (19% from fat); PRO 2g; FAT 4g (sat 2.3g); CARB 40g; FIB 0.8g; CHOL 0mg; IRON 0.6mg; SOD 74mg; CALC 2mg

Pear, Walnut, and Maple Syrup Pie

Comice pears work best, but almost any variety can be used. Toasting the walnuts imparts a deep nutty flavor that contrasts with the maple syrup.

2 cups all-purpose flour, divided
⅓ cup ice water
½ teaspoon salt
3 tablespoons chilled butter or stick margarine, cut into small pieces
3 tablespoons vegetable shortening
4 large Comice pears (about 3 pounds), peeled, cored, and cut into ½-inch-thick wedges
1 tablespoon lemon juice
¼ cup pure maple syrup
1 teaspoon vanilla extract
⅓ cup firmly packed brown sugar
⅓ cup chopped walnuts, toasted
3 tablespoons cornstarch
Cooking spray
2 teaspoons water
1 large egg

1. Combine ⅓ cup flour and ice water in a small bowl, stirring with a whisk until well blended. Combine remaining 1⅔ cups flour and salt in a medium bowl; cut in butter and shortening with a pastry blender or 2 knives until mixture resembles coarse meal. Add ice water mixture; toss with a fork until moist. Divide dough in half. Gently press each half of dough into a 4-inch circle on heavy-duty plastic wrap; cover with additional

plastic wrap. Roll one half of dough, still covered, into a 12-inch circle; freeze 10 minutes. Roll other half of dough, still covered, into an 11-inch circle; freeze 10 minutes.

2. Preheat oven to 450°.

3. Combine pears and lemon juice in a large bowl; toss gently. Add syrup and vanilla, and toss gently. Add brown sugar, walnuts, and cornstarch; stir well.

4. Remove plastic wrap from 12-inch circle of dough, and fit dough into a 9-inch pie plate coated with cooking spray, allowing dough to extend over edge of plate. Combine 2 teaspoons water and egg in a small bowl; stir well with a whisk. Spoon pear mixture into prepared crust, and brush edges of piecrust lightly with egg mixture. Remove plastic wrap from 11-inch circle of dough, and place dough on top of pear mixture. Press edges of dough together; fold edges under, and flute.

5. Brush top and edges of pie with egg mixture. Place pie on a baking sheet; cut 5 (1-inch) slits into top of pastry using a sharp knife. Bake at 450° for 15 minutes. Reduce oven temperature to 350° (do not remove pie from oven); bake an additional 45 minutes or until browned. Let cool on a wire rack 30 minutes. Serve warm or at room temperature. Yield: 10 servings.

POINTS: 6; **Diabetic Exchanges:** 2 Starch, 1½ Fat, 1 Fruit
Per serving: CAL 290 (31% from fat); PRO 5g; FAT 10g (sat 1g); CARB 47g; FIB 3.1g; CHOL 22mg; IRON 1.8mg; SOD 168mg; CALC 30mg

MEASURING STICKY INGREDIENTS:

When measuring honey, molasses, syrup, or other sticky ingredients, first coat the measuring spoon or liquid measuring cup with cooking spray. Then the ingredient will slip out easily and cleanup will be simple.

Pear, Walnut, and Maple Syrup Pie brings a taste of New England to your dinner table.

Oatmeal-Spice Cookies

Plum Betty

We found that this betty, which contains layered fruit, sugar, breadcrumbs, and cookie crumbs, is even better when served warm with vanilla low-fat ice cream.

5   cups sliced plums (about 1½ pounds)
⅔   cup sugar
3   tablespoons apple juice
½   teaspoon ground cinnamon
¾   cup fresh breadcrumbs
¾   cup soft oatmeal-raisin cookie crumbs
    (about 3 cookies, such as Archway)
2   tablespoons butter or stick margarine, melted
Cooking spray

1. Preheat oven to 350°.

2. Combine first 4 ingredients in a bowl; toss gently.

3. Combine breadcrumbs, cookie crumbs, and butter in bowl; toss with a fork. Sprinkle ⅓ cup breadcrumb mixture into bottom of a 1½-quart casserole coated with cooking spray. Top with half of plum mixture; sprinkle with ⅓ cup breadcrumb mixture. Top with remaining plum mixture; sprinkle with remaining breadcrumb mixture. Cover and bake at 350° for 35 minutes. Uncover; bake an additional 15 minutes or until bubbly. Yield: 6 servings (serving size: ¾ cup).

POINTS: 5; **Diabetic Exchanges:** 2½ Starch, 1 Fruit, ½ Fat
Per serving: CAL 274 (23% from fat); PRO 3g; FAT 7g (sat 1.3g); CARB 54g; FIB 3.4g; CHOL 2.7mg; IRON 0.9mg; SOD 131mg; CALC 14mg

Oatmeal-Spice Cookies

Generous amounts of cinnamon, nutmeg, and ginger give this cookie its spicy kick. If you prefer a milder flavor, you can cut the amount of spices in half. Store cookies in an airtight container for up to one week.

1½ cups all-purpose flour
1   teaspoon baking soda
1   teaspoon ground cinnamon
1   teaspoon ground nutmeg
½   teaspoon salt
½   teaspoon ground ginger
1   cup firmly packed brown sugar
½   cup granulated sugar
½   cup butter or stick margarine, softened
3   tablespoons light-colored corn syrup
1½ teaspoons vanilla extract
2   large egg whites
1   large egg
3   cups quick-cooking oats
1⅓ cups raisins
Cooking spray

1. Preheat oven to 350°.

2. Combine first 6 ingredients in a small bowl; stir well, and set aside. Combine brown sugar and next 6 ingredients in a large bowl; beat at medium speed of a mixer until well blended. Stir in oats and raisins; let stand 5 minutes. Stir in flour mixture.

3. Drop dough by level tablespoons 2 inches apart onto baking sheets coated with cooking spray. Bake at 350° for 10 minutes or until lightly browned. Remove cookies from pans, and let cool on wire racks. Yield: 4½ dozen (serving size: 1 cookie).

POINTS: 2; **Diabetic Exchanges:** 1 Starch
Per serving: CAL 79 (23% from fat); PRO 2g; FAT 2g (sat 0.4g); CARB 14g; FIB 0.8g; CHOL 4mg; IRON 0.5mg; SOD 71mg; CALC 9mg

MEASURING BROWN SUGAR:

To measure accurately, use the dry measuring cup that holds the exact amount of brown sugar called for in a recipe. Pack sugar firmly into the cup; then level it off. The sugar will hold its shape when turned out of the cup.

Turtle Cupcakes

Caramel oozes from the center of these cupcakes.

1   (1-pound, 4.5-ounce) package
      low-fat fudge brownie mix
¼   cup finely chopped pecans
Cooking spray
⅓   cup fat-free caramel-flavored ice cream
      topping (such as Smucker's)

1. Preheat oven to 350°.

2. Prepare brownie batter according to package directions; stir in pecans.

3. Place paper baking cups in muffin pans, and coat with cooking spray. Divide half of batter evenly among baking cups. Spoon 1 teaspoon caramel topping into center of each cupcake. In each cup, drop 1 teaspoon batter from tip of a spoon, guiding the dripping batter around the outside edge of caramel topping. Top evenly with remaining batter. Bake at 350° for 25 minutes. Remove cupcakes from pans, and let cool completely on wire racks. Yield: 16 servings (serving size: 1 cupcake).

POINTS: 4; **Diabetic Exchanges:** 2 Starch, 1 Fat
Per serving: CAL 194 (19% from fat); PRO 2g; FAT 4g (sat 0.7g); CARB 36g; FIB 1.3g; CHOL 0mg; IRON 2.5mg; SOD 73mg; CALC 9mg

Bananas Foster

1   tablespoon butter or stick margarine
4   bananas, quartered
¼   cup firmly packed dark brown sugar
¼   cup banana liqueur
⅛   teaspoon ground cinnamon
¼   cup dark rum
2   cups vanilla fat-free frozen yogurt

1. Melt butter in a large skillet over medium-high heat. Add bananas and next 3 ingredients; cook 2 minutes or until tender, stirring constantly.

2. Pour rum over bananas, and ignite with a long match; cook until flames disappear. Spoon ½ cup yogurt into each of 4 bowls; top evenly with banana mixture. Yield: 4 servings.

POINTS: 5; **Diabetic Exchanges:** 2 Starch, 2 Fruit
Per serving: CAL 285 (11% from fat); PRO 3.7g; FAT 3.5g (sat 2g); CARB 62.8g; FIB 2.8g; CHOL 8mg; IRON 0.6mg; SOD 75mg; CALC 91mg

Irish Cream-Espresso Crème Caramel

The experience of a silky smooth, sweet spoonful of crème caramel melting in your mouth is unforgettable.

⅓   cup sugar
3   tablespoons water
Cooking spray
2   large eggs
1   large egg white
1   (12-ounce) can evaporated fat-free milk
½   cup sugar
1   tablespoon instant espresso or 2 tablespoons
      instant coffee granules
3   tablespoons Irish cream (such as Bailey's)
⅛   teaspoon salt
Chopped chocolate-covered coffee
      beans (optional)

1. Preheat oven to 325°.

2. Combine ⅓ cup sugar and 3 tablespoons water in a small, heavy saucepan. Place over medium-high heat, and cook until sugar dissolves, stirring frequently. Continue cooking until golden (about 4 minutes). Immediately pour into 4 (6-ounce) ramekins or custard cups coated with cooking spray, tilting each cup quickly until caramelized sugar coats bottom of cup. Set aside.

3. Beat eggs and egg white in a medium bowl with a whisk. Add milk, ½ cup sugar, espresso, Irish cream, and salt; stir until well blended. Divide mixture evenly among prepared ramekins. Place ramekins in a 9-inch square baking pan; add hot water to pan to a depth of 1 inch. Bake at 325° for 55 minutes or until a knife inserted in center comes out clean. Remove ramekins from pan; let cool. Cover and chill at least 4 hours. Loosen edges of custards with a knife or rubber spatula. Place a dessert plate, upside down, on top of each ramekin; invert onto plates. Drizzle any remaining caramelized syrup over custards. Garnish with chopped coffee beans, if desired. Yield: 4 servings.

POINTS: 7; **Diabetic Exchanges:** 3 Starch, ½ Sk Milk, ½ Fat
Per serving: CAL 305 (15% from fat); PRO 11g; FAT 5g (sat 2g); CARB 55g; FIB 0g; CHOL 114mg; IRON 0.7mg; SOD 229mg; CALC 264mg

Irish Cream-Espresso
Crème Caramel

Creamy Rice Pudding

There's no need to reserve this dish for dessert only—try it for breakfast, too. You can speed up the recipe by cooking it over medium heat rather than low, but you'll need to stir it constantly.

4   cups whole milk
1   cup uncooked long-grain rice
½   teaspoon salt
½   cup sugar
½   cup half-and-half
1   teaspoon ground cinnamon
4   large egg yolks, lightly beaten
1   cup raisins
1½ teaspoons vanilla extract

1. Combine first 3 ingredients in a medium saucepan; bring to a simmer over medium heat, stirring constantly. Cover, reduce heat to low, and cook 30 minutes or until rice is tender, stirring occasionally.

2. Combine sugar and next 3 ingredients in a small bowl; stir well with a whisk. Gradually stir about one-fourth of hot milk mixture into egg yolk mixture; add yolk mixture to remaining hot milk mixture. Place over low heat, and cook 3 minutes or until mixture reaches 160° and is thick and bubbly, stirring constantly. Stir in raisins and vanilla. Serve warm or chilled. Yield: 10 servings (serving size: ½ cup).

POINTS: 6; **Diabetic Exchanges:** 2½ Starch, ½ Wh Milk
Per serving: CAL 255 (25% from fat); PRO 6g; FAT 7g (sat 3.6g); CARB 42g; FIB 0.9g; CHOL 105mg; IRON 1.5mg; SOD 176mg; CALC 153mg

Peach Ice Cream

Use peaches that are fragrant and ripe. They'll be easy to mash and will impart a perfumy aroma.

1½ cups sugar, divided
2   cups peeled mashed fresh peaches
5   large eggs
1   (14-ounce) can sweetened condensed milk
1   (12-ounce) can evaporated milk
1   tablespoon vanilla extract
5   cups whole milk

1. Combine ½ cup sugar and peaches in a bowl; stir well, and set aside.

2. Place eggs in a medium bowl; beat at medium speed of a mixer until frothy. Add remaining 1 cup sugar; beat well. Add condensed milk and evaporated milk; beat well. Pour into a large, heavy saucepan; bring to a boil over medium heat, and cook 1 minute, stirring constantly. Remove from heat; stir in vanilla. Let cool completely. Stir peach mixture into cooled milk mixture.

3. Pour peach mixture and whole milk into the freezer can of an ice cream freezer; freeze according to manufacturer's instructions. Spoon ice cream into a freezer-safe container; cover and freeze 1 hour or until firm. Yield: 16 servings (serving size: 1 cup).

POINTS: 6; **Diabetic Exchanges:** 2½ Starch, ½ Wh Milk
Per serving: CAL 266 (27% from fat); PRO 8g; FAT 8g (sat 2g); CARB 41g; FIB 0.4g; CHOL 93mg; IRON 0.3mg; SOD 111mg; CALC 164mg

MEASURING LIQUID INGREDIENTS:

Measure liquids on a level surface in a glass or clear plastic measuring cup with a pouring lip. Read liquid measurements at eye level.

Old-Fashioned Gingerbread

Top this traditional molasses-spice cake with a dollop of store-bought lemon curd or whipped topping.

Cooking spray
2   teaspoons all-purpose flour
½   cup butter or stick margarine, softened
1   cup sugar
1   cup molasses
1   large egg
2½ cups all-purpose flour

1½ teaspoons baking soda
1   teaspoon ground ginger
1   teaspoon ground cinnamon
½   teaspoon salt
1   cup hot water

1. Preheat oven to 350°.

2. Coat a 13- x 9-inch baking pan with cooking spray; dust with 2 teaspoons flour. Set aside.

3. Place butter in a large bowl; beat at medium speed of a mixer until creamy. Gradually add sugar; beat well. Add molasses and egg; beat well. Combine 2½ cups flour and next 4 ingredients; stir well. Add flour mixture to creamed mixture alternately with hot water, beginning and ending with flour mixture.

4. Pour batter into prepared pan. Bake at 350° for 35 minutes or until a wooden pick inserted in center comes out clean. Let cool slightly in pan on a wire rack. Serve warm or at room temperature. Yield: 15 servings.

POINTS: 5; **Diabetic Exchanges:** 3 Starch, ½ Fat
Per serving: CAL 242 (26% from fat); PRO 3g; FAT 7g (sat 4g); CARB 44g; FIB 0.6g; CHOL 31mg; IRON 2.1mg; SOD 236mg; CALC 53mg

Tiramisu Angel Torte

3   (8-ounce) cartons plain fat-free yogurt
1   cup sugar, divided
½   cup water
2   tablespoons instant espresso or ¼ cup instant coffee granules
2   tablespoons Kahlúa (coffee-flavored liqueur)
1   (4-ounce) carton mascarpone cheese
2   tablespoons fat-free milk
½   teaspoon vanilla extract
2   tablespoons unsweetened cocoa
1   ounce bittersweet chocolate, grated (about ⅓ cup)
1   (10-inch) round angel food cake

1. Place a colander in a 2-quart glass measure or medium bowl. Line colander with 4 layers of cheesecloth, allowing cheesecloth to extend over outside edges. Spoon yogurt into colander. Cover loosely with plastic wrap; refrigerate 2 hours. Spoon yogurt cheese into a bowl; discard liquid. Cover and chill.

2. Combine ½ cup sugar, water, and espresso granules in a small saucepan; bring to a boil over medium heat, and cook 1 minute, stirring occasionally. Remove from heat; stir in Kahlúa. Let cool completely.

3. Combine yogurt cheese, remaining ½ cup sugar, mascarpone cheese, milk, and vanilla; beat at medium speed of a mixer until smooth. Set cheese mixture aside.

4. Combine cocoa and grated chocolate in a small bowl; stir well, and set aside. Cut angel food cake into 12 slices using a serrated knife. Dip cake slices into espresso mixture; place 4 slices in the bottom of a 9- x 5-inch loaf pan. Gently spread one-third of cheese mixture over cake layer, and sprinkle with one-third of cocoa mixture. Repeat procedure with remaining cake slices, cheese mixture, and cocoa mixture. Cover and chill at least 2 hours. Yield: 10 servings (serving size: ¾ cup).

POINTS: 6; **Diabetic Exchanges:** 2½ Starch, ½ Sk Milk, ½ V-L Meat, ½ Fat
Per serving: CAL 290 (22% from fat); PRO 16g; FAT 7g (sat 3.4g); CARB 47.2g; FIB 0g; CHOL 10mg; IRON 0.4mg; SOD 223mg; CALC 225mg

Tiramisu Angel Torte combines coffee-Kahlúa soaked cake with chocolate and creamy, sweet cheese.

Red Velvet Cake

This cake has half the fat of its traditional namesake. Our Test Kitchens staff was divided on what kind of frosting is best on it. One side had memories of a Cream Cheese Frosting, while the other insisted that Cooked Buttercream Frosting makes it a true Red Velvet Cake. What follows is the buttercream version.

Cooking spray
1   tablespoon all-purpose flour
1⅔ cups granulated sugar
5   tablespoons vegetable shortening
1   large egg white
1   large egg
3   tablespoons unsweetened cocoa
1   (1-ounce) bottle red food coloring
2¼ cups all-purpose flour
1   teaspoon salt
1   cup low-fat buttermilk
1¼ teaspoons vanilla extract
1   tablespoon white vinegar
1   teaspoon baking soda
Cooked Buttercream Frosting

1. Preheat oven to 350°.

2. Coat 2 (9-inch) round cake pans with cooking spray, and dust with 1 tablespoon flour. Set aside.

3. Beat sugar and shortening at medium speed of a mixer 5 minutes or until well blended. Add egg white and egg; beat well. Combine cocoa and food coloring in a small bowl; stir well with a whisk. Add to sugar mixture; beat well.

4. Combine flour and salt. Add flour mixture to sugar mixture alternately with buttermilk, beginning and ending with flour mixture. Add vanilla; beat well. Combine vinegar and baking soda in a small bowl; add to batter, beating well.

5. Pour batter into prepared pans. Sharply tap pans once on counter to remove air bubbles. Bake at 350° for 28 minutes or until a wooden pick inserted in center comes out clean. Let cool in pans 10 minutes; remove from pans. Let cool completely on wire racks.

6. Place 1 cake layer on a cake plate; spread with ⅓ cup Cooked Buttercream Frosting, and top with remaining cake layer. Spread remaining frosting over top and sides of cake. Store cake loosely covered in refrigerator. Yield: 16 servings.

POINTS: 7; **Diabetic Exchanges:** 4 Starch, 1 Fat
Per serving: CAL 322 (25% from fat); PRO 5g; FAT 9g (sat 3.3g); CARB 58g; FIB 0.6g; CHOL 30mg; IRON 1.3mg; SOD 310mg; CALC 44mg

Cooked Buttercream Frosting:

Don't substitute margarine for the light butter in this recipe. The texture and taste of the frosting will not be the same.

7   tablespoons all-purpose flour
1   cup fat-free milk
12 tablespoons chilled light stick butter (such as Land O'Lakes)
2½ cups powdered sugar (do not sift)
1   teaspoon vanilla extract

The delicate taste and texture of Red Velvet Cake comes from a combination of not-too-sweet ingredients.

1. Place flour in a small, heavy saucepan. Gradually add milk, stirring with a whisk until well blended. Place over medium heat, and cook 2½ minutes or until very thick, stirring constantly with whisk. Spoon into a bowl; cover and chill thoroughly.

2. Beat chilled butter and chilled flour mixture at medium speed of a mixer until smooth. Gradually add powdered sugar, and beat just until blended (do not overbeat). Stir in vanilla; cover and chill. Yield: 2⅓ cups.

Peanut Butter and Chocolate Thins

1½ cups all-purpose flour
¾ cup firmly packed brown sugar
¼ teaspoon salt
3 tablespoons chilled butter or stick margarine, cut into small pieces
2 teaspoons vanilla extract
1 large egg, lightly beaten
Cooking spray
½ cup semisweet chocolate chips
3 tablespoons reduced-fat crunchy peanut butter

1. Preheat oven to 375°.

2. Combine first 3 ingredients in a medium bowl. Cut in margarine with a pastry blender or 2 knives until mixture resembles coarse crumbs. Stir in vanilla and egg.

3. Pat dough into a 13- x 9-inch baking pan coated with cooking spray. Bake at 375° for 10 minutes. Remove from oven; let cool completely on a wire rack.

4. Combine chocolate chips and peanut butter in a small saucepan. Place over medium heat, and cook until mixture melts, stirring constantly. Spread chocolate mixture over crust; cover and chill at least 1 hour. Cut into 24 bars. Store in refrigerator in an airtight container. Yield: 2 dozen (serving size: 1 bar).

POINTS: 2; **Diabetic Exchanges:** 1 Starch, ½ Fat
Per serving: CAL 101 (36% from fat); PRO 2g; FAT 4g (sat 1.2g); CARB 16g; FIB 0.4g; CHOL 9mg; IRON 0.6mg; SOD 56mg; CALC 9mg

MEASURING DRY INGREDIENTS:

The correct measuring technique is critical to the success of low-fat baked goods. With less fat, there is less room for error, particularly when measuring flour. It's important to get in the habit of measuring ingredients with precision.

Use stainless steel or plastic dry measuring cups. First, stir the flour several times with a spoon. Then, lightly spoon the flour into the appropriate cup until it mounds slightly.

Level the top using a straight-edged spatula or knife. Do not tap cup.

BREAKFAST

Garlic-Cheese Grits (page 18), ¾ cup
poached egg, 1
orange, 1
Total **POINTS**: 6

Open-Faced Apple-Cheese Bagels
   (page 26), ½ bagel
fat-free milk, 1 cup
orange juice, ½ cup
Total **POINTS**: 7

Poached Fruit (page 14), ½ cup fruit and
   about 2 tablespoons yogurt mixture
whole wheat English muffin, toasted, 1
fat-free milk, 1 cup
Total **POINTS**: 8

Glazed Cinnamon-Orange Biscuits (page
   18), 2 biscuits
apple, 1
vanilla fat-free aspartame-sweetened yogurt,
   8 ounces
Total **POINTS**: 7

Marmalade-Broiled Grapefruit (page 13),
   ½ grapefruit
Crunchy Granola (page 26), ½ cup
fat-free milk, 1 cup
Total **POINTS**: 7

Fresh Apple Coffee Cake (page 18),
   1 slice
cantaloupe, ¼ melon
fat-free milk, 1 cup
Total **POINTS**: 7

Sausage Breakfast Casserole (page 21), 1
   serving
high-fiber whole wheat toast, 1 slice
Brunch Ambrosia (page 22), 1 cup fruit
   mixture and 1 teaspoon coconut
Spicy Virgin Mary (page 21), 1 cup
Total **POINTS**: 6

LUNCH

Chicken Noodle Soup (page 36), 1 cup
saltines, 6
banana, 1
fat-free milk, 1 cup
Total **POINTS**: 9

Smoked-Salmon Sandwiches (page 46), 1
carrot sticks, 1 cup
Hummus (page 49), ½ cup
Total **POINTS**: 9

Turkey-in-the-Slaw Sandwiches
   (page 37), 1
Crunchy Snack Mix (page 39), 1 cup
apple, 1
Total **POINTS**: 10

Zesty Double-Bean Salad (page 39), 1 cup
cheese toast: 1 slice high-fiber whole wheat
   bread with 3 tablespoons shredded
   cheddar cheese
pear, 1
Mississippi Mud Brownies (page 82), 1
Total **POINTS**: 9

Greek Spaghetti With Tomatoes and Feta
   (page 49), 1¼ cups
crisp breadsticks, 2 long
apple, 1
Total **POINTS**: 9

Curried Tofu-Egg Salad Sandwiches
   (page 45), 1
Cucumber Vichyssoise (page 40), 1 cup
seedless grapes, 1 cup
Total **POINTS**: 9

Jamaican Shrimp-and-Rice Salad (page
   42), 2 cups
sweet potato chips (such as Terra Chips), 1
   ounce
Total **POINTS**: 11

DINNER

Artichoke-Pepper Pizza With Feta Cheese
   (page 62), 1 wedge
green salad, 1 cup, with 2 tablespoons fat-
   free Italian dressing
Lemon Bars (page 78), 1
Total **POINTS**: 9

Peppered Lamb Chops (page 61),
   1 serving
Baked Mushroom Rice (page 71), 1 cup
steamed broccoli, 1 cup
Total **POINTS**: 10

Parmesan-Breaded Tofu Marinara (page
   66), 1 serving
steamed asparagus, 12 spears
Oatmeal-Spice Cookies (page 85), 1
Total **POINTS**: 12

Pesto-Topped Orange Roughy (page 57),
   1 serving
cooked couscous, 1 cup
steamed baby carrots, 1 cup
Pineapple Sherbet (page 75), ½ cup
Total **POINTS**: 10

Greek Pork Tenderloin Salad (page 56), 1
   serving
Plum Betty (page 85), ¾ cup
Total **POINTS**: 10

Triple-Corn Spoon Bread (page 57), 1
   serving
baked pork chop, 1
steamed green beans, 1 cup
Total **POINTS**: 9

Fettuccine Alfredo (page 54), 1 cup
Tossed Salad Supreme (page 53), 2 cups
Total **POINTS**: 8

Here are specific guidelines that *Weight Watchers* Magazine adheres to regarding our recipes. To ensure nutritional accuracy, we recommend that you follow these suggestions.

• When preparing a recipe that yields more than one serving, be sure to mix the ingredients well, and then divide the mixture evenly.

• Where liquid and solid parts have to be divided evenly, drain the liquid and set it aside. Evenly divide the remaining ingredients, and then add equal amounts of the liquid to each serving.

• Unless otherwise indicated, servings of meat, poultry, and fish refer to cooked, skinned, and boned servings.

• Recipes provide approximate nutritional information, including the following: CAL (calories), PRO (protein), FAT (total fat), sat (saturated fat), CARB (carbohydrates), FIB (dietary fiber), CHOL (cholesterol), IRON (iron), SOD (sodium), and CALC (calcium). Measurements are abbreviated as follows: g (grams), mg (milligrams).

• Recipes include **POINTS**® based on Weight Watchers International's 1•2•3 Success® Weight Loss Plan.

• *POINTS* are calculated from a formula based on calories, fat, and fiber that assigns higher points to higher-calorie, higher-fat foods. Based on your present weight, you are allowed a certain number of *POINTS* per day.

Note: Because data on fat distribution are not available for some processed foods, these breakdowns should be considered approximate.

• Recipes include diabetic exchanges, which are calculated from the *Exchange List for Meal Planning* developed by the American Dietetic Association and the American Diabetes Association. The exchange information is designated as follows: starch, fruit, sk milk (skim milk), l-f milk (low-fat milk), wh milk (whole milk), veg (vegetable), v-l meat (very lean meat), l meat (lean meat), m-f meat (medium-fat meat), h-f meat (high-fat meat), and fat.

Each category from the exchange list consists of foods that are similar in their nutritional makeup. Therefore, foods within the same category can be substituted. For example, ½ cup cereal for one slice of bread.

• The recipes that are shown in our photographs may vary as to the number of servings pictured. For accuracy, please refer to the recipes for the exact serving information.

B A K I N G P A N S U B S T I T U T I O N S

Shape	Dimensions	Capacity	Substitutions
Rectangular	11- x 7- x 1½-inch	8 cups	8- x 8- x 2-inch
	13- x 9- x 2-inch	12 to 15 cups	two 9-inch round or three 8-inch round
Square	8- x 8- x 2-inch	8 cups	11- x 7- x 1½-inch
	9- x 9- x 2-inch	10 cups	9- x 5- x 3-inch loaf pan or two 8-inch round
Round	8- x 1½-inch	5 cups	10- x 6- x 2-inch
	8- x 2-inch	6 cups	8½- x 4½- x 2½-inch loaf pan
	9- x 1½-inch	6 cups	8- x 2-inch round
Tube	10- x 4-inch	16 cups	10-inch ring mold or cake mold
Loaf	8½- x 4½- x 2½-inch	6 cups	two or three 6- x 3- x 2-inch loaf pans
	9- x 5- x 3-inch	8 cups	three or four 6- x 3- x 2-inch loaf pans
Pie plate	9- x 1½-inch	5 cups	No substitution unless tart pans are used
	10- x 1½-inch	6 cups	
Jelly-roll pan	15- x 10- x 1-inch	10 cups	Do not substitute baking sheet for jelly-roll pan

IN THE FREEZER
(at -10° to 0°)

Dairy

Cheese, hard	3 months
Cheese, soft	2 weeks
Egg substitute	6 months
Egg whites	6 months
Egg yolks	8 months
Ice cream, sherbet	1 month

Fruits and Vegetables

Commercially frozen fruits	1 year
Commercially frozen vegetables	8 to 12 months

Meats, Poultry, and Seafood

Beef, Lamb, and Veal

Ground, uncooked, and all cuts, cooked	3 months
Roasts and steaks, uncooked	9 months

Pork

Ground, uncooked, and all cuts, cooked	3 months
Roasts and chops, uncooked	6 months

Poultry

All cuts, cooked	1 month
Boned or bone-in pieces, uncooked	6 months

Seafood

Perch, trout, and shellfish	3 months
Cod, flounder, and halibut	6 months

IN THE REFRIGERATOR
(at 34° to 40°)

Dairy

Butter and margarine	1 month
Buttermilk, low-fat	1 to 2 weeks
Cheese, grated Parmesan	1 year
Cheeses, cheddar and Swiss	3 to 4 weeks
Cream cheese, ⅓-less-fat, light, and fat-free	2 weeks
Eggs and egg substitute	1 month

Meats, Poultry, and Seafood

Beef, Lamb, Pork, and Veal

Ground and stew meat, uncooked	1 to 2 days
Roasts, uncooked	2 to 4 days
Steaks and chops, uncooked	3 to 5 days

Chicken, Turkey, and Seafood

All cuts, uncooked	1 to 2 days

Fruits and Vegetables

Apples, beets, cabbage, carrots, celery, citrus fruits, and parsnips	2 to 3 weeks
Apricots, berries, peaches, pears, plums, asparagus, cauliflower, cucumbers, mushrooms, okra, peas, peppers, salad greens, and summer squash	2 to 4 days
Corn, husked	1 day

IN THE PANTRY
Keep these at room temperature
for six to 12 months.

Baking and Cooking Supplies

Baking powder
Biscuit and baking mix
Broth, canned
Cooking spray
Honey
Mayonnaise, light, low-fat, and
   fat-free (unopened)
Milk, canned evaporated fat-free
Milk, fat-free dry
Mustard, prepared (unopened)
Oils, olive and vegetable
Pasta, dried
Peanut butter, regular and reduced-fat
Rice, instant and regular
Salad dressings, bottled (unopened)
Seasoning sauces, bottled
Tuna, canned

Fruits, Legumes, and Vegetables

Fruits, canned
Legumes (beans, lentils, peas),
   dried or canned
Tomato products, canned
Vegetables, canned

E Q U I V A L E N T   M E A S U R E S

3	teaspoons	1	tablespoon
4	tablespoons	¼	cup
5⅓	tablespoons	⅓	cup
8	tablespoons	½	cup
16	tablespoons	1	cup
2	tablespoons (liquid)	1	ounce
1	cup	8	fluid ounces

2	cups	1	pint (16 fluid ounces)
4	cups	1	quart
4	quarts	1	gallon
⅛	cup	2	tablespoons
⅓	cup	5	tablespoons plus 1 teaspoon
⅔	cup	10	tablespoons plus 2 teaspoons
¾	cup	12	tablespoons